GREENER PASTURES

From Bombay and Boston to the Bulls and Bears

Matthew Gallagher with Brian Culp

ISBN: 1973917165
ISBN 13: 9781973917168
Library of Congress Control Number: 2017912073
CreateSpace Independent Publishing Platform
North Charleston, South Carolina

Advisory services offered through Change Path, LLC and Investment Advisor. Gallagher Financial Group and Change Path, LLC are not affiliated.

The material is not intended to be legal or tax advice. The presenter can provide information, but not advice related to social security benefits. Clients should seek guidance from the Social Security Administration regarding their particular situation. Annuities are products of the insurance industry; guarantees are backed by the claims-paying ability of the issuing company. Guaranteed lifetime income available through annuitization or the purchase of an optional lifetime income rider, a benefit for which an annual premium is charged.

TABLE OF CONTENTS

ACKNOWLEDGEMENT

This book is dedicated to my wonderfully supportive family: My wife, Erica, and my boys, Jaden and Jensen. They are the best teammates on this journey that I could have ever asked for and they keep me laughing and loving every moment of my life. Also to my dad who much of this book focuses on, from our business and personal relationships, to the many life lessons that he taught me along the way. And to my mom, even though I don't share a lot about her in the following pages since this book is about our business, she has been the rock behind the scenes for me my entire life. I can always count on her to be there no matter what I need. And she has never let me down. Her prayers are why I am here today. And last but not least, I want to thank God for giving me ability and opportunity to write this book.

PREFACE

I wrote this book because I felt like there are way too many financial "text books" out there. The average individual finds them tough to read unless it's a substitute for sleeping pills. People feel like they are being talked down to or feel the author is condescending. I'm even a CFP® practitioner and I often feel that way myself reading that garbage. So, I wanted to write a book that simply shared entertaining but true stories from my own life with a financial parallel that just might help you in making your own retirement decisions. And I do hope you find this both enjoyable and enlightening. But if you find it neither, please give it to one of your smarter friends so that they can explain it to you and then you both can have a laugh. (Kidding - But be prepared, this book will keep you on your toes where sarcasm is concerned.) Thanks for taking the time to make me and my life part of your library of knowledge. God Bless!

1

FROM BACK TO THE FUTURE

The person on top of the mountain didn't just fall there.

—Vince Lombardi

There are many reasons I decided to get into the financial-planning business and then become a Certified Financial Planner™ practitioner. First and foremost, I grew up in this business. I was fascinated watching how my dad related to people. I remember going on appointments with him after school, sitting in clients' living rooms, and observing how they interacted. He definitely had—and still has—the gift of empathy. In addition, every day is a new challenge and a new adventure. Almost every day, I get to teach something new about how our economy works, how our world works, and how people work.

Over the years, however, I've come to realize that there's much more to my profession than that. I've come to realize that money—how it's invested and what happens as it shapes our lives—functions more like a passport. Money is a tool. A means to an end. A vehicle in which we move our lives from point A to point B.

And as someone who considers myself mainly an extrovert, being in the financial business helps me get to know people. Every day I re-connect with existing clients and get to meet others for the very first time. That's the part of the job I love most. In fact, I spend the majority of my days *not* hunched over a computer monitor trying to divine some hidden market-timing strategy or picking stocks; instead, I spend nearly all day every day talking. And listening. I get to ask clients about their families, about their hopes, their fears, and their goals. I take great satisfaction knowing I've had a part in helping these folks on a path to achieving some of their hopes and reaching their goals, while steering them away from their fears.

Perhaps the biggest reason why I got into the financial-planning business is one that's as old as time: Dad. Growing up, I watched my father build his own career, and thus work toward his own hopes and dreams by helping people pursue their own financial goals. Although I couldn't really put it into words while I was growing up, the reason why I admired my dad so much, and part of the reason why I want this book to pay tribute to his legacy in some small way, was that I was watching someone make the world a better place.

Dad helped people plan and afford educations for their kids, dream vacations for themselves, and charitable giving, the impact of which will leave a legacy to be passed on for generations to come. My story of getting into the financial-planning business, then, is a story of watching someone make the world a better place to live, one day and one person at a time.

But he is not without his detractors. Like most people I know, he has had his share of misfortune. Goodness knows we all have. What's more, Dad's public-radio persona has meant that some of these stumbles have become fodder for the press. I want to discuss this topic head on, right here at the outset. I can tell you without reservation that my father is an honest, devout family man whose driving motivation in life is to help Americans have a guaranteed income they can't outlive. My father always taught me to persevere when challenges arose, to admit errors and grow from them as a result (in chapter 4, you'll get a great sense of how Dad put this principle in action), and to strive every day to make the world a better place, despite what others may say or write. Even if those things that are written are grotesque exaggerations or complete fabrications. The truth is that people always love to try and tear down those who are on top. And because of his work ethic and sincere love for others, Dad has been on top for many, many years. And that is why some of these pay-for-play publications have tried to unsuccessfully attack him. They envy the attention and headlines. You would know them today simply as "Fake News."

As is the case with countless sons and fathers all over the world, I draw inspiration from my dad. So, just like many other fathers and sons, I've followed in his footsteps and have stepped into the family business.

But here's the funny thing about my dad—well, one of them, anyway: he's better known by a nickname most commonly associated not with the financial-advising business but with the medical profession.

My father is William Neil Gallagher. However, from the time I was eight months old, I've known him simply as Dad. I say, "from the time I was eight months," and not "for as long as I can remember," because I was eight months old when W. Neil and Gail Gallagher, while he was working as a pastor (his profession before he became a financial advisor) in East Providence, Rhode Island, adopted me from an orphanage in Bombay, India.

Of course, other than my two brothers and two sisters, I'm the only one who gets to call him Dad. And around the offices of the Gallagher Financial Group, I have that privilege all to myself. The *other* people who know Dad best—his friends, his clients, and the folks who listen to his weekly radio programs—know him better by another name altogether, a nickname he's used for the last forty years or so: "Doc."

When someone adds value to your life, well then, that person proves to be a great investment. And great investments are worth a lifetime. They require little to be maintained but give you plenty in return.

—Robin Sacredfire

The Gallagher Chronicle

He is not called Doc without reason, mind you. W. Neil Gallagher— or Dad—holds a PhD in Philosophy with a concentration in Ethics from Brown University, which he received in 1980. He and Gail started their lives together in 1966, when Dad worked as a minister to a small congregation.

Then, during the early summer of 1985, with a new addition to the family buckled into the back seat, Dad and Mom picked up and moved to Memphis, Tennessee, and embarked on a major life change for our family. (There were a few other stops along the way between Rhode Island and Tennessee—such was a pastor's life back then.) Doc Gallagher left the ministry and became a financial planner at Dean Witter. Four short years later, we moved to Texas (upon arrival, of course, Dad picked up a pair of cowboy boots), where he worked for AG Edwards and then eventually left the big Wall Street firms and hung his own shingle in the Dallas–Fort Worth area. Doc started an independent advisory firm and named it the Gallagher Financial Group. He built and ran that company for a little over thirty-two years, and he still serves as the owner and CEO/resident to this day.

And that's not all in Doc's resume. During his thirty-two years guiding the Gallagher Financial Group, he authored over seventy articles in professional journals and magazines and somehow found the time to write no fewer than fifteen books—and counting. (As someone who only now understands the time and resources needed to complete just one book, that's a feat that I don't see myself matching anytime soon. A man's got to sleep, after all!) He also traveled extensively to speak at motivational seminars hosted by his friend Zig Ziglar.

And of course, he's been on the radio for an hour (or three) nearly each and every Thursday, Saturday, and Sunday on stations all over central Texas. Doc's original broadcasts began hitting the airwaves starting back in 1997 and continue to this day. These days, I join Dad for one of the main Saturday programs.

I guess what I'm saying is that it's been quite a life for W. Neil "Doc" Gallagher, and I feel grateful to have shared in that life.

Through it all, Dad has taught me the values of hard work, perseverance, resolve, patience, forgiveness, and the importance of faith in informing day-to-day decisions about work and life. But there's been one lesson above all the others that Doc Gallagher has passed along to his adopted son. It's the one that's made the most lasting impression on how I run the business now and will continue to run the business until the day when it's time to pass along the practice to someone else, maybe even one (or both) of my own sons.

The lesson is a simple one: The Gallagher Group isn't really in the finance business. The Gallagher Group is in **the people business.**

So Why Did I Write This Book, Anyway?
Anyone starting out on a book project should first be able to answer that fundamental question, or else he or she shouldn't bother writing a book in the first place. (Did I mention that writing a book is a lot of work?) For you to understand what guides my core philosophies on financial planning, you should first understand a few things about me. (Did I mention that we're in the people business?) About my faith. About my adoption and childhood. About my family. And about some of the significant moments in my life that have helped shape me as a person, which in turn have shaped my advice as a Certified Financial Planner™ practitioner.

It takes as much energy to wish as it does to plan.

—Eleanor Roosevelt

Not Me and Someday
We'll have the rest of the book to discuss these matters. In the nine chapters that follow, you'll gain a bit of insight (make that a *lot* of insight) into who I am, and why I make the financial recommendations that I do. I'll also have time to share several thoughts about where *not* to invest your hard-earned dollars.

In this introductory chapter, however, I want to tell you a quick story about the two clients whom we visit with almost every day at the Gallagher Financial Group:

1. The Not Me client
2. The Someday client

Of course, these two clients are personifications of the *types* of clients we tend to see week in and week out at the Gallagher Financial Group. They are also the two types of clients *most* in need of a sound financial planning.

To put some real, actual numbers behind our two hypothetical clients, know that the Gallagher Financial Group welcomes in somewhere in the neighborhood of a few thousand people through its doors every single year. As you might expect, some of these people are existing clients. They are dropping by to say hello, or to make a deposit, or to add a beneficiary, or to make a withdrawal, or sometimes just to hear me rant about the Rangers, Mavs, Stars, or Cowboys (the Rangers are due this year, by the way), the teams of my adopted hometown. Or they came to hear me *really* rant about the Red Sox, Celtics, Bruins, and Patriots, the teams of my childhood home. (Readers who have visited my office can attest to the Boston-based sports memorabilia decorating the walls.)

In any event, many of these thousands of visitors are new guests to our firm. They are prospective clients, walking through our doors, who are only just starting out in pursuit of their goals. Some of these folks are young men and women—some still single, some newlyweds, some with children, some not—who are embarking on their careers, their families, and their future lives.

Of this majority of prospects we see, many become new clients of the Gallagher Financial Group. Some do not. But seeing brand new clients, or at least young people who might become new clients, doesn't surprise me. I *expect* that most young people will be seeking out advice when they are just getting out of high school or college, and are starting to make a full-time salary for the first time in their lives.

However, most of the folks walking through the doors of the GFG are *not* just starting out. Most are experienced investors with ten, twenty, thirty years or more of putting money away for retirement under their collective belts. In fact, I'd estimate that about 75 percent of our new clients every year *already have a financial plan in place.*

Given that's the case, here's what *still* amazes me even after doing this for over twelve years: how many of the Gallagher Financial Group's new clients have an existing plan that, unfortunately, isn't working out. How many clients are considering switching their financial advisors and placing their retirement goals in the Gallagher Financial Group.

These people didn't make the decision to walk through our doors lightly; they're mulling over a big decision in their lives. These experienced investors are now thinking about transferring their assets, their life savings, their plans and hopes for their future, and in many cases, their plans and hopes for their children's and grandchildren's future.

And I'm happy to report that most of these "old" prospective investors eventually become clients of the Gallagher Financial Group. And they do so after hearing, in one form or another, much of the advice and anecdotes contained throughout this book.

But not all prospects thinking about switching end up making the switch. And what I've learned is that it never truly comes down to how much time I spend with these types of potential clients. I can spend minutes, ten hours, or ten days going over a detailed financial strategy of investing. I can present hours' worth of facts and figures about historical market returns and financial downturns and bond interest rates and the like. I can essentially recite this entire book, filled with sound advice about how to reliably grow parts of their portfolio over the long stretch, and shield other parts of their portfolio from unnecessary risk.

And what surprises me even more is that these same people usually *agree* with every single part of the plan. They know it's solid advice. Indeed, it's advice they may have gotten from elsewhere, listening to other advisors, and by reading other books. I certainly don't have a monopoly on quality financial planning, just like the personal trainer doesn't have the market cornered on how to become physically fit. A personal trainer's real job is to make you do all those push-up and cardio sessions that you know are good for you but that you don't want to do. The personal trainer keeps you *accountable*.

But just like the person who has the goal to lose weight but can't be bothered to get to the gym, these same prospects will express their desire to achieve their financial goals, and nod their head when I show them how to achieve their financial goals, but they just don't take the most crucial step of all when it comes to investing:

They don't act.

What keeps them from acting? From getting down to the financial CrossFit gym, as it were? It always comes down to two excuses. You guessed it:

Not Me and *Someday.*

It's not hard to tell these two types of clients apart. The Not Me clients, when it's time to act to shore up their investments or remove portfolio risk, are certain that the investment pitfalls that can affect other portfolios can't possibly impact their own. The Not Me prospects have convinced themselves that market crashes like the ones in 2001 and 2008 are for other people. Every single person who lost money in each of the downturns of '01 and '08 thinks that his or her investments won't go down again. And he or she is right—until the moment they do.

The Someday client is also easy to spot. The Someday clients are the ones who nod their head, the ones who always ask good follow-up questions. The Someday clients seem to be the kind of people who make a bold New Year's resolution to get to the gym and then decide the best time to start that gym membership is right about January 15, right after the big crowds have died down. In other words, they'll start their workout routine *someday*.

As with the someday gym-goers who will be starting, they promise, after January 15, the Someday financial planners have their investment future all plotted out and will start that new journey *someday*... just after tax season or once summer starts or when the kids go back to school or right after the holidays. The hallmark of the Someday client is the innate ability to procrastinate.

(In my opinion, the Someday clients are the more dangerous of the two, as they typically have fooled themselves into thinking they will take action...but just not now. In the case of the Not Me folks, they at least have a chance one day to realize that, yes, it *could* be them!)

There are virtually no guarantees in the financial-planning business, but here are two you can absolutely, positively bank on: one is that money stuffed in a mattress will earn exactly 0 percent in interest. The other is that neither the Not Me nor the Someday folks have a terribly good chance of achieving their financial objectives.

But as I've mentioned, I learned a lot from watching my dad run his business for the past thirty-two plus years. And another lesson that has really hit home for me is that helping one person at a time means just that. We cannot serve the investment needs of all of Texas, or even the entire Dallas/Ft. Worth area. And in this world, despite our best efforts, some people we meet will be Not Me prospects, and some will be Someday clients.

Is There an Ocean in Fort Worth? A Metaphorical Ocean, Maybe
It's like that old story about the brother and sister, and the sad sight of thousands of starfish swept up on the beach after a storm. When the girl bent to pick up one of the thousands of starfish, the boy said to her, "What are you doing? There are thousands more still stranded on this beach. What difference will it make?" The sister hurled the starfish back in the water and said to her brother, "It made a difference to that one!"

So, the Gallagher Financial Group has long ago made peace with the fact that we can't help all the starfish on all the world's beaches. But (if you'll allow me to extend the metaphor) we can help one. And then we can help another. And then one more. And by doing that day after day, week after week, and year after year, we can help a whole lot of starfish get back to the places God meant for them to be.

So, this book is for those of you who may feel stranded on a financial beach, or for those of you who might be wondering, "Hey, is this a beach? And is that the ocean? And if starfish don't have eyes and ears or brains, how can they possibly tell the difference? Because I kind of feel like a starfish when it comes to finances." (OK, so I've extended the metaphor just a bit further).

If that describes your situation, then I think you'll find a lot of value in the pages to come. Here's what you can expect in the next nine chapters. Hopefully, after reading through what follows you'll take the necessary actions to move you along the course of finding your own personal waters of financial peace and stability.

> In **chapter 2,** we'll kick off the discussion of financial-planning matters with a story about a sweet, four-year-old boy and his piggy bank. It's about how on one beautiful spring day, the sweet four-year-old threatened a reign of destruction upon those around him over the thought of losing the money in said piggy bank.

Chapter 3 will tell you (almost) everything you wanted to know about house foundations, and how that relates to financial planning.

Chapter 4 is all about facing your fears. It's about a scary car wreck I was in that still gives me nightmares. And it's about what you can learn from a car wreck to help you invest more wisely.

Chapter 5 will discuss everyone's favorite topic—cookies. Well, at least it's my favorite topic anyway. The chapter is also about food. And about how sometimes people make permanent-retirement decisions based on their stomach.

Chapter 6 is about how misunderstandings can lead to bad investment decisions. It's about my interview process with new clients, which allows me to advise from a place of being well informed. It's also about a line from *Angry Birds*. Sort of. You'll see.

In **chapter 7,** you'll briefly hear about my exploits in the game of hockey to try and encourage my oldest son, who started playing, and how that relates to timing the market, and how both are bad ideas. It's about how one of those ideas in particular is a *terrible* idea that can end up sabotaging even the best-laid retirement plan.

Chapter 8 touches on the idea of safety. It explores the things we do to feel safe in our homes and in our retirements, and how sometimes a *feeling* of safety is not the same thing as *actual* safety. You'll also read a description of me wearing only red shorts and waving around a souvenir kiddie baseball bat. You've been warned.

Chapter 9 contains a rather detailed description of the Post-it notes covering my wife's mirror, and how it relates to the bigger picture of investing, domestic harmony, and building a life of wealth. It will make sense once you read it. You'll just have to go with me on this one for now.

Chapter 10 is about returning home. About going back to the people and places that serve as the anchor points, both in life and in a retirement plan. It's about the people behind the Gallagher Financial Group, and the events that have shaped their lives and their advice to clients.

So, go grab a cup of coffee, or pour yourself a cup of tea, or pop the top of a Guinness or two. I've designed this book to get right to the point, and most readers should be able to digest it in just a sitting or two. The reason? It's mostly because, as I mentioned previously, much of the financial advice most people should follow doesn't take all that long to explain.

By the time we reach the end, I will have laid out a path to financial success that will work for the vast majority of those saving for their retirement. Hopefully at that time, you'll consider hiring me to serve as your guide on that path.

But much, much, much more importantly: I hope that you decide to *start the journey on that path.* If you do that, I'll consider this book a rousing success, because it will have helped one person—you.

One person at a time. Exactly as Doc showed me.

2

PROTECTING YOUR PIG

*The average 65-year-old woman today can be
expected to live to 86, a man to 84. One out of
10 people who are 65 today will live past 95.*

—*Official Statistic, Social Security Administration.*

I f you're reading this chapter in search of a specific piece of financial advice, or a suggestion about asset classes, I'll begin with a bit of fair warning: you're probably better off skipping ahead. (If you're waiting for the chapter where I recommend parking your assets in gold or cash, some additional warning: you're probably better off finding another book.)

Because more than anything else, this chapter about a *mind-set.*

Yet it's this mind-set that could be more important than any suggestion I make in these pages about how to reliably grow your wealth, or what pitfalls to avoid that can wreak havoc on the average investor.

And to help get you in that mind-set, I'll first tell you about a kid.

A Brief Ode to 7-Eleven Nachos
That kid is me.

In the previous chapter, I mentioned that I've been in the financial business for twelve years now. And that's *mostly* correct. After graduating from Baylor (Sic 'em Bears!) and while working at the Gallagher Financial Group, I went on to earn a couple of postgraduate certificates. In 2009, I received a Certificate in Financial Planning from SMU. Then, in 2014, I received my Certificate in Executive Management from Notre Dame (Wake up the echoes!).

But it all started back in 2006 with Farmers Financial Services. After being a captive planner for a year, I followed in my dad's footsteps by becoming independent. I began my journey with the Gallagher Financial Group in 2007, and by 2012 I had earned my CFP® designation. Ever since then, I have been blessed to have Certified Financial Planner™ practitioner on everything from my business cards to my tax returns.

But you got most of that professional background stuff already.

However, there's another part of the story I left out.

My very, *very* first job in the financial world started when I was seven years old. It began with what we'll call—hmm, how do we say this?—an "internship" with my father, Doc Gallagher.

As touched on previously, I learned a lot during those childhood years, even though I didn't fully realize it at the time. The following are some examples:

While I was filling my after-school time, weekends, and summers filing papers to help out, I witnessed Dad create lasting relationships with people he had not met until the moment they stepped through his office doors. While I was tied up answering phones, I observed him tied up in meetings where he showed empathy to new clients, listening carefully before taking even the first steps toward offering advice. Even if that meant turning the occasional person away, Dad always wanted to make sure that he did right by them. And during that time, I learned that this business is about establishing relationships and showing dedication even more than it is about establishing accounts and building portfolios.

It's not about numbers on a spreadsheet, it's about people.

But remember, I was a kid. I was seven years old while soaking up all this information the way a sponge soaks up water. During that time, my favorite part of the financial-planning business was the job of planning the late-night trips to 7-Eleven so I could get nachos— lots of chili and cheese sauce, extra jalapeno peppers, of course— and a big Slurpee. To a scruffy kid, this is all the payment he ever requires. Thus, properly fueled with sugar, chili, and cheese (three of the four official Texas food groups, I believe) from the after-hours snack run, Dad and I would oftentimes head over to the ball fields near the client's home we had gone to that night and catch a baseball or softball game. We didn't know the teams. We didn't care. It was a wonderful ending to each night's time together that had begun with Dad helping people reach their retirement goals from their dinner table. Despite the late nights for such a young boy, us spending that time together will always be a wonderful memory instead of being left home for the evening while Dad was gone working hard to support our family. It is the same type of memories that I want to share with my boys someday as well.

During those visits to clients and attendance at ballgames, I was of course focused mainly on what flavor of Slurpee I was having that night. Subconsciously, though, I was learning valuable lessons. I learned that sometimes business isn't done at 5:00 p.m. each day, and that sometimes the business of serving clients means being available on *their* schedule, not on ours.

That faith. That dedication. That integrity. That perseverance. Those are principles I learned following Dad around all those many sweltering summer nights in Dallas-Fort Worth and many times beyond.

And it also reminds me of a popular song.

The Child Is the Father
Actually, not a popular *song* per se, but rather an obscure song from a popular *band*.

The band is the Beach Boys, and there's a song buried deep in their discography called "The Child Is the Father of the Man." The tune certainly isn't as famous or as catchy as other Beach Boys classics like "California Girls" or "Good Vibrations," but the title of that song resonated with me from the moment I heard it. You'll see why as we continue.

And, as someone pointed out one time when I was talking about this song and how it relates to investing, the title in fact derives from a rather famous *poem*. For those of you with a more literary background, you might have already recognized it: the poem is a work from a poet named William Wordsworth, called "My Heart Leaps Up." (The line about the child being the father of the man is like the seventh line, although don't worry, this won't be on the test.)

The meaning of this line is extremely profound—at least it is for me. Like all great art, there are several possible interpretations (the entire poem and a brief critical analysis is available at *Wikipedia*), and therefore what meaning you take away from the poem, or the painting, or the photograph, can serve as commentary on both artist and observer.

In any event, my interpretation of "the child is the father of the man" is that a man is a by-product of the habits and values developed in them when the adult is a child.

In other words, the lessons learned either by listening to or observing parents and teachers during the formative years are just that—formative. A child who grows up with parents who love classical piano music tend to develop a love for music him- or herself. A child who observes his or her parents donating time and resources to charitable causes is likely to develop a deeper sense of empathy and stewardship.

And in my case, a child who grows up loving baseball games and nachos and will grow up to love the sounds and smells of Friday evenings at Globe Life Park in Arlington, which remind him of summer nights spent watching his beloved Boston Red Sox. That child will also develop a set of fundamental traits. Traits that have made me who I am: A sense of empathy and stewardship for our client's resources. An abiding faith. A loyalty and love for my family.

You see? The child is the father of the man.

The Child Has a Piggy Bank
And that gets us to the mind-set part of this tale.

I have two sons, Jaden and Jensen, who are now six and three at the time of writing this. The story I'm about to share is about Jaden, and more specifically, about a possession that he fell in love with when he was four years old.

More specifically than *that*, it's about how Jaden's love of the possession in question can help us all develop what I consider a very necessary mind-set as we approach our retirement years.

It's about Jaden's piggy bank. Or at least it's about the piggy bank I bought him one fall shortly after he turned four and had expressed a desire to save up all the coins that he would find in the parking lots or on the ground pretty much anywhere. Searching for coins became as much of a game to him as baseball or checkers—the object of the game wasn't even necessarily to find cash others had let fall to the earth. For him, it was more about the hunt for treasure. He especially loved looking for coins while he was out with his Nana (my mom who I've talked about previously)—which is exactly what Nana had done with *her* Nanny many years before.

Now, then, as many four-year-olds do, Jaden loved Thomas the Train. Did I say "loved"? I meant *loooved*. If there were such a thing as super-powered italics, I'd have used them in that last sentence.

In any event, when I first brought home the new piggy bank, Jaden went absolutely crazy over it. We're talking new-bicycle-on-Christmas-morning levels of excitement here. Erica and I congratulated ourselves for our superior gifting skills, because we had combined what we observed were Jaden's two obsessions: first, Thomas the Train. Obviously. Secondly, money!

Naturally, seeing Jaden's excitement over the Thomas the Train piggy bank set the old steam engine of my imagination down a certain track. I began thinking that the rush of excitement Jaden felt over receiving the piggy bank is familiar to many investors, especially those investors who are nearing retirement age.

> *Saving is a great habit but without investing and tracking, it just sleeps.*

—Manoj Arora, From the Rat Race to Financial Freedom

The Piggy Bank When You're Four Score and Four.
Of course, some of the piggy banks we grown-up types deal with don't look much like Thomas the Train. Hopefully. Instead, they resemble 401(k)s, or IRAs, or brokerage accounts. Some even look simply like a savings account kept somewhere in a local bank. (Keep in mind that in terms of interest earned, there's essentially no difference between a savings account and a Thomas the Train piggy bank. I'm just kidding. Or am I?) Us adult types spend, or have spent, much of our lifetimes trying to build up the biggest piggy bank we can create.

For most, putting as much as we can into our piggy banks seems like a goal that's so obvious that it's not even worth discussing. We want an overflowing piggy bank so that we can have the life we want in our retirement years. We want to enjoy the world and our grand-kids and every moment we have left without becoming a burden on others or having others feed and clothe us. That's the whole point of "feeding the pig," isn't it?

But what happens once that bank is filled?

Ah, there's the rub. We focus so hard to fill our retirement ac-counts that we may lose sight of the work of protecting that pig—that very pig we're going to depend on to feed us for years to come. It's just like in football when the coach tells the star running back to hold onto the "pigskin" tightly and not to fumble with it. The coach is concerned with him "protecting that pig" because a single fumble can cost his team the entire game. In investing, a "fumble" could cost someone their ability to retire, their flexibility to travel to see their grandchildren, or even their entire retirement savings, forcing them to go on welfare or move in with their kids to make ends meet. And I haven't met anyone who wants to become a burden to their children. Instead, they want to be able to help them and leave some type of a legacy or inheritance to them. So, what are some of the best ways to protect that pig we've worked so hard for?

The first step is to develop the proper mind-set.

This brings us back to my son, Jaden.

The child does not want you to touch his piggy bank. Like never, ever.

At first, Jaden loved (*loooved*) his piggy bank for what it was on the outside—he loved (*loooved*) seeing his favorite Thomas character on top of his nightstand every morning when he got out of bed, and he even made sure to tell the piggy bank goodnight before going to bed.

Over time, however, Thomas became fat with money. Spare change from a trip to the store. One dollar and five dollar bills for helping out Erica and me around the house—some additional funds earned in return for filling up our sweet dog, Hailee's water bowl. A few quarters for emptying the trash in his room or feeding his Beta fish, James. You get the idea.

And now that Thomas was filled with Jaden's very own money, he became even more excited about his piggy bank because of what it was on the *inside*. For Jaden, the stuff on the inside of his bank took on a different meaning—it wasn't simply a pile of coins and folded-up green paper. For Jaden, this represented his dreams. It represented *possibility*. It represented the chance to someday walk into a Toys"R"Us and buy a Thomas the Train wooden railway set. Or a video game. It represented the freedom to walk into a 7-Eleven and get a supersized Slurpee and not have to ask permission from Dad. (But only one per day…who am I kidding? I'd probably let him have a few hundred but then Erica would kill me when I got home.)

In some small way, that piggy bank represented an ability for Jaden to exercise *control* over his own life. That Thomas was his ticket to endless possibilities.

Sounds familiar?

Erica and I took pride in watching Jaden become more and more excited about the piggy bank. Excited and also protective. Protective as in, "If anyone would be so foolish as to come in and, ahem, *borrow* money from Thomas the Train, Jaden will unleash a reign of punishment the likes of which the world has never seen." Believe me, this is something that no human being wants to see. Jaden can go head-to-head with the best of them as it is; the thought of losing the contents of Thomas is capable of sending young Jaden into molten-hot rage. And I don't blame him!

Why? Because the idea of losing what's in Thomas is *just as powerful* as the idea *should* be to most retirees over losing what's in their own personal piggy banks. Because Jaden doesn't want to lose what he's worked so hard to save.

No one is going to take anything out of Jaden's Thomas the Train bank. Neither Erica nor I would dare such a move; we've become quite fond of having our hands and fingers attached, thank you very much.

Unfortunately, many retirees don't take all the precautions that four-year-old Jaden Gallagher does with his piggy bank. For Jaden, it's easy to protect the pig. Nothing bad will happen to the pig because it's off limits to everyone except him. But bad things can, and do, happen with adult piggy banks, mostly because they are not as easy to keep on top of a nightstand. They can be—and oftentimes are—exposed to swings of the stock market, to interest rates, and to the effects of inflation, just to name a few.

For example, in a *U.S. News* report, Emily Brandon cites the Congressional Budget Office reporting that stock-market turmoil wiped out roughly $2 trillion of Americans' retirement savings during a fifteen-month period in 2007 through 2008. That's a lot of Thomas the Trains. That's a staggering loss we've had to endure in just one market correction.

The Child is the Father. Again.

But the first step in developing the proper mind-set to protect our adult piggy banks is to first come to terms with the fact that no matter how smart we are, no matter how much information we ingest, we are powerless to control the forces that can harm our "pig." Similar to the first step in Alcoholics Anonymous, which states "we admitted that we were powerless over alcohol—that our lives had become unmanageable," many investors today still need to admit that they are powerless over market, interest rate, and outside conditions that affect our hard-earned dollars. And to those who cannot come to terms with that, their portfolios and retirement often become unmanageable. Most of the folks I've spoken with, who are considering switching their retirement accounts to the Gallagher Financial Group spent countless hours watching CNBC during the last great market downturn—and the market tanked anyway. Therefore, the only thing we can do is leverage the tools at our disposal to protect that pig.

And to help us act, it helps to regain that mind-set that we perhaps held when we were children, and receiving our very own piggy bank for the first time. We must remember that these numbers on paper are as real as if we were holding the cash in our hands, and we must be willing to protect what is rightfully ours, to keep what we deserve.

Finally, we must be open to seeking out the counsel and wisdom of others. Of course, this means having a conversation with someone like me, someone who deals with adult piggy banks day in and day out, someone who can take your emotions over your retirement savings and shape them into a plan that will help protect those savings. And I don't particularly care if the licensed financial advisor you seek out is me. It's my hope that this book will be read far and wide, and there are only so many hours in my day, of which I always carve some out for my family.

But no matter what, use that *mind-set* to your advantage. Seek out a professional who can help you look at different protection methods that may be suitable for you and help you get on—and stay on—the path you desire.

An investment in knowledge pays the best interest.

—Benjamin Franklin

In summary, we could all use a little more of Jaden's steadfast attitude when it comes to protecting our piggy bank. For us to enjoy the retirement piggy bank we have worked so hard for, we must first get into the right frame of mind about protecting that piggy bank in the first place. And no, I'm not saying every dollar you earn must be kept from market risk nor am I recommending any particular investments.

And thus, the theme repeats once more:

> When it comes to developing the right *mind-set* needed for our retirement, we would do well to allow the child—in this case my child Jaden—to become the father of the man.

3

MY FOUNDATIONAL WISDOM

*I believe that the biggest mistake that most people make
when it comes to their retirement is they do not plan
for it. They take the same route as Alice in the story
from "Alice in Wonderland," in which the cat tells
Alice that surely she will get somewhere as long as she
walks long enough. It may not be exactly where you
wanted to get to, but you certainly get somewhere.*

—Mark Singer, *The Changing Landscape Of
Retirement—What You Don't Know Could Hurt You*

I'm not sure what geological challenges you face in your part of
the country, or your part of the world (I have a vision of a reader
or two perusing this book from a beachside cabana in Cabo or
Fiji or somewhere), but here in the hot, dusty, Dallas/Fort Worth me-
troplex, we have *terrible* problems with foundations. Over time, they,
too, succumb to the pressures of time and weather, and if not taken
care of properly, they too will become part of the red, cracked, dusty
clay that's under our feet.

Foundations. Important when planning construction on a house.
Equally as important when mapping out a retirement plan. That's
why I spend a lot of time in my financial practice talking about the

foundations that underpin the structures, which provide both our literal and our financial support.

The foundation principle

Some say it's the heat. Or the cold. Or it could be the extreme swings in temperature between the summer and winter months down here in the dusty plains. I'm not entirely sure. What I do know is that the summers down here are generally dry and *mucho caliente*. We're talking habanero sauce, cook-an-egg-on-the-sidewalk hot. The winters down here, meanwhile, are also generally dry and scorching hot, at least when compared to winters, say, in Green Bay, Wisconsin or Thunder Bay, Ontario, Canada. (Impressed that a Texan knows his Canadian Provinces? I thought so.)

But, we do also get our share of Green-Bay-like cold snaps, when temperatures in the December through January months will dip into the mid-twenties, and stay that way for about week or two. Believe it or not, we even get *snow* in Texas every once in a while. And ice. Bad ice. And Texas drivers, well…never mind, I'm getting sidetracked.

As I said, I'm not sure of the exact cause. I'm neither a geologist nor a meteorologist.

What I *do* know is what general contractors who build houses for a living (some of whom are clients of the Gallagher Financial Group) tell me all the time: *foundation* problems are a massive, massive concern down here in the Lone Star State. In fact, these same folks tell me that a *majority* of the houses in the area will eventually need foundation repair.

I probably don't need to spend much time going over the numbers associated with a foundation repair. If there are two words that can turn the dream home into the stuff of nightmares more quickly than any other, especially when it comes time to sell that dream home, it's the two words "structural inspection." Not that I'm speaking from experience or anything. Wait a minute—yes, I am.

In any event, here's the one number that sticks with me when foundation repairs come up during conversation:

Eleven gabillion.

Now that I think about it, that may just be what the number *sounds* like to my ears. That may just be me trying to process numbers like $40,000, $60,000, $80,000, or more and then comparing that to the overall mortgage on the house. Whatever the actual number is, all of us homeowners know that foundation issues can sometimes mean repair costs that run into the many tens of thousands.

In short, it's no exaggeration to say that having to repair a broken foundation can mean the loss of nearly *half* of the home's value.

❧

So, what does all this talk of foundations have to do with retirement planning?

I'm sure you can already spot the financial parallels. When it comes time to retire, *we need a strong foundation on which to build further financial success.* In other words, our financial "house" should rest on something that's solid and stable; something that isn't prone to wobble, crack, or worse collapse. You want your financial house resting on solid rock, and not on shifting sand.

The reasons why should be fairly obvious. As we approach retirement age and will depend on those dollars we've saved up over our lifetimes, the risks to having a shaky financial foundation are simply too great. After all, we wouldn't want a "crack" in our financial house to cost us half of that house's value when it comes time to enjoy our retirement savings.

Why? Because unlike hiring a foundation-repair specialist to come out and install reinforcing beams to address the situation in a matter of days, there usually isn't enough *time* to address a financial foundation that has turned to dust. (And if we *do* try to make those "repairs" in a matter of days, we find ourselves in things that can quickly lead us down the path of further financial collapse: buying stocks on margin, counting cards at a blackjack table, or heck, even robbing a bank. Unless you're a character in a movie, I don't recommend any of these financial options.)

In other words, we can throw *money* at a foundation problem when that foundation problem is under the first floor of our house. However, what's needed to restore a broken portfolio foundation is *time*. And as we all know, time is a commodity that's always in short supply.

So what does a solid foundation look like in terms of investing, then?

For many of my clients, it looks like an *annuity*.

Behold the Annuity

For most of my clients, an annuity serves as a good foundation to their retirement savings. It can be the part of a retirement plan that sets your financial house atop a rock-solid footing, and provides a complement to the overall retirement plan. In fact, for many of my clients, the conservative financial objectives expressed through annuities provide the freedom to seek more aggressive returns with other parts of their portfolios.

As you will hear me say throughout the book, smart retirement planning is all about finding the right *balance* in your financial picture. Annuities can be just the thing that makes the balancing act possible. And let me say this from the outset: *no* portfolio should ever be 100 percent invested in an annuity. If you meet with a financial advisor who recommends this approach, my advice is that you politely shake his or her hand, thank him or her for the appointment, and then *sprint* for the doors as fast as you can. That advisor does not have your best interests at heart. I also want to make it clear that I am *not* saying that everyone should own an annuity. *If* an annuity is appropriate for an individual based on his or her needs and goals, then it often becomes part of protecting the financial foundation that we are discussing here.

Opposed to those planners who want to put all of a client's money in annuities, there are those who want to invest the entire amount in the stock market regardless of that client's risk tolerance or objectives. I don't believe this is right either. Both are extremes and as we all have learned wisely over the years, extremes should usually be avoided. I do want you to know this—I have the best interests of all my clients at heart. It's the core philosophy around which the Gallagher Financial Group has been built. What's more, as a Certified Financial Planner™ practitioner, I have a duty to put your financial objectives (to protect your capital, grow your assets, etc.) in front of mine (to make sure the firm turns a profit, to grow the business, etc.). That's why I will sometimes recommend annuities as a *part* of your overall investment pie, when suitable—just not the entire pie.

♆

Digging Deep into the Details on Annuities

With that said, let's first understand some of the key concepts behind annuities. Armed with this understanding, I think you'll agree with some of my conclusions when it comes to using annuities to create a solid financial foundation.

According to the website Investopedia (a portmanteau of *Investing* and *Encyclopedia*—get it?), an "annuity" is "a contractual financial product sold by financial institutions that is designed to accept and grow funds from an individual and then, upon annuitization, pay out a stream of payments to the individual at a later point in time."

(By the way, *Investopedia* is a sort-of *Wikipedia* for investing, where you can look up lots of financial terms and concepts. It also includes a portfolio tracking tool for those who are so inclined. It's a fantastic resource for those looking for quick definitions about investment products.)

The important part of that rather wordy definition are the words *pay out a stream of payments to the individual.* In other words, an annuity is a series of payments. Those payments can be weekly, monthly, quarterly, or annually. Heck, annuities can be written so that the payments are made every time there's a full moon. I've never seen this, mind you, but it is *possible.* What the annuity requires is that the payment occurs at a regular interval of time. (No, we don't and won't sell moon-phase-based annuities at the GFG, even though I agree that might be a cool thing, so please don't ask.)

What's more, almost everyone who sets up an account at the Gallagher Financial Group has already had an annuity most of their adult lives. What am I talking about? Your mortgage. That's right, a monthly mortgage payment is actually a form of an annuity. A mortgage is annuitized on the closing date, when all the mortgage papers are signed.

Pensions are annuities, too. So is Social Security. Social Security is just an annuity the government purchases for us (technically, the government makes us purchase the annuity by collecting payroll taxes throughout our working lives), and then pays retirees monthly payments until they pass away.

When it comes to the types of annuities that I recommend as the foundation for a typical client of the Gallagher Financial Group, they vary depending on the client's needs from ones that defer payments while protecting principal to others that pay an immediate income stream to cover current expenses. They are one tool (of many that we may recommend, depending on your needs, wants, and goals) available to help make sure retirees don't outlive their retirement assets.

So, at its heart, an annuity purchase is very simple—the individual purchases a product. What product does he or she purchases? Monthly deposits into your bank account either now or at a later date (or even a lump-sum deposit should you want that with a deferred annuity—but that's another topic we can discuss in person should you choose). What's more, those monthly deposits are *set in stone*. And they can provide an income that *you can't outlive*. They serve as the foundation for all else that's part of your investing portfolio.

Be the Wise Builder
A couple of times in this chapter, I've mentioned that purchasing an annuity can be like setting your financial foundation on a rock. (In fact, you may have noticed the phrase *set in stone* in the previous paragraph was italicized.)

You're about to learn the reason I've used that specific reference.

In the Bible, there's a parable that has proven to be so instructive that it makes two separate appearances in the Gospels. The first time is in the Book of Matthew (that would be the Book *of* Matthew, not this book *by* Matthew), and the second mention happens during the Book of Luke. It's the parable of the Wise and the Foolish Builder. In fact, the story resonates so profoundly that it's familiar to many who aren't familiar with the Bible. And for those who are, there was probably a song about this that you learned very early in life.

The story illustrates the importance of building one's life upon a solid foundation. In the story of the Wise and the Foolish Builder, the foundation referenced is the teachings of Jesus.

Here is the relevant excerpt from the book of Matthew, with the emphasis mine:

> *Everyone therefore who hears these words of mine, and does them, I will liken him to **a wise man, who built his house on a rock.** The rain came down, the floods came, and the winds blew, and beat on **that house; and it didn't fall, for it was founded on the rock.** Everyone who hears these words of mine, and doesn't do them will be like **a foolish man, who built his house on the sand.** The rain came down, the floods came, and the winds blew, and beat on **that house; and it fell—and great was its fall.***

When the parable is weaved into the narrative of Luke, there's language used that I like even better. Again, the emphasis is mine.

> *Everyone who comes to me and hears my words and does them, I will show you what he is like: **he is like a man building a house, who dug deep and laid the foundation on the rock. And when a flood arose, the stream broke against that house and could not shake it,** because it had been well built. But the one who hears and does not do them is like a man **who built a house on the ground without a foundation. When the stream broke against it, immediately it fell, and the ruin of that house was great.***

The meaning of the Wise and Foolish Builder parable is both powerful and straightforward. In fact, it is such a powerful metaphor, applicable to so many of life's challenges, losses, and ills, that it has been woven into numerous songs and hymns and stories, and now, into a book discussing sound financial principles.

And it's something I stress to clients and potential clients of the Gallagher Financial Group almost every day, several times a day (hey, if it's a good enough parable to be used twice in the Bible, then it's good enough to be referenced multiple times a day while dispensing financial advice). When it comes to your retirement, I want you to build your portfolio of investments by *digging deep.*

When that financial flood comes, in whatever form it might take—an unexpected medical bill, a job loss, a crash in housing values, market downturns, and so forth—I want to make sure your financial house remains standing. I want you to *dig deep* with your portfolio—I want it anchored into something that will not shake you financially—so that it doesn't waver under the shifting sands of the economy.

Make Sure Your Foundation is Rock-solid.

Let's close our discussion of foundations with a definition that should even more drive home the importance of this chapter. The word I want you to remember is *cornerstone*. What exactly is a cornerstone? A cornerstone, also known as a *foundation stone,* is the very *first* stone in a foundation that all the other stones are built upon. If this stone isn't right, the rest of the foundation will not be set right either, which therefore means neither will the rest of the structure. It is imperative that a builder gets the cornerstone right. And that's *exactly* what I do. I build your financial house, your financial foundation, but most importantly I set your financial cornerstone properly in place so that anything we build on it will not fall.

And what if whoever you've worked with in the past or currently are with has not set the appropriate cornerstone or foundation for your retirement plan? Well, it can be a catastrophically bad plan if, one year from now, two years from now, or seven years from now, we get a repeat of 2008. Don't remember '08? Well, let me be the first to welcome you back to planet Earth. What was the weather like in that alternate dimension, and did the Rangers win the World Series? Did they get that final strike—twice? (Yeah, that one hurts me too—still.)

For the rest of you, I'm betting that you're probably trying to remember whether you lost 30 percent or 35 percent of your investment value back in '08. And if so, let me extend to you some hearty congratulations, because *you beat the market during that period!* **During the 2008 bear market, the average investor lost 38 percent.**

In my role as a financial advisor, I want to make sure that if you're working at Starbucks into your seventies, it's because you *really* love coffee, and want to spend the day talking with people, and making Unicorn Frappuccino's (it's a thing), and not because you're trying to figure out how to make ends meet.

And most of all, I don't want to see anyone come home from a long day of making pink-and-blue coffee drinks, settle in to his or her most comfortable chair, turn on the TV…and then have the wall the TV is mounted to collapse on itself because the wall is sitting atop a shaky foundation.

You won't be able to make enough Unicorn Frappuccinos to pay for a major foundation repair, and you certainly can't reach your retirement goals unless you first make sure that retirement portfolio rests on a solid *foundation.*

As with house foundations, your financial foundation should be rock solid, and can be with the right financial advisor in place. And I am that advisor.

4

MATTHEW'S REASONS TO FEAR NOT

Face the thing you fear the most.

—Doc Gallagher

I t all started with a Mercedes Benz. Specifically, it's about a bright red Mercedes Benz. A very cool car. For some, owning a Mercedes is symbolic. It's a statement that the owner has achieved some measure of financial success or professional accomplishment. Sometimes, owning a Mercedes is a way to impress a potential client. Or a means of making the daily commute a bit more comfortable. Or simply a reward for a job done well.

But this is not a story about the status a Mercedes bestows on its owner. It is not a discussion about whether or not one can or should purchase a brand-new Mercedes or about the front-end safety features or about retention of resale value or about the interest rate of a loan or about the wisdom of buying new versus used or about at what point in our investing or professional lives we've saved up enough that we *deserve* a Mercedes.

In fact, the Mercedes story really has nothing to do with automobiles at all.

It's about fear.

The Mercedes Accident Story

The year was 1995. May 1995 to be exact. I was fifteen years old. I had just received my learner's permit after a semester of taking the Driver's Ed course at Fort Worth Christian High School. And after a year of near-continuous begging my parents about driving me down to the DMV so I could sit for the test, I was able to drive. Well, drive with a licensed adult.

While I had spent the early part of the 1990s terrorizing elementary and junior high playgrounds, Dad had spent the same time building up the Gallagher Financial Group from the ground floor—from having a single solitary client, unsure about how he would pay the following month's office rent, to a large, thriving financial-services firm that employed a lot of people.

So, in the mid-90s, Dad finally bought the first luxury vehicle he had ever purchased in his life: a bright, shiny red Mercedes. Leather seats. Sunroof. Power everything. Connection to a cell phone so Dad could check in with the office or catch up with a client while driving back and forth across Interstates 30 or 35. (Remember, this was a time where people were just starting to use cell phones. A phone hooked up to the car speakers was a very big deal. Actually, they were known as car phones back then.) In every way, this new Mercedes was Doc's dream car.

At the very same time, Dad bought my mom, Gail, a brand-new Toyota Camry. It was a bit more toned down in terms of the luxury features—cloth seats instead of leather, for example, but the blue-green Camry was a nice new vehicle nonetheless. And it was exactly what she had wanted. Nothing too flashy but something pretty that drove like a dream.

So, to quickly recap: In May 1995, I was part of a household that included two brand-spanking-new automobiles; and I was a fifteen-year-old who had just gotten his permit to drive a few months before that.

I know what you're thinking, and you're right; probably a prescription for disaster if there ever was one.

If you recall the days of having a learner's permit to drive, then you recall that it's one step down from a restricted driver's license, which allows teenagers to drive to and from work or school. In contrast, a learner's permit allows a teen requires pretty much anywhere, with the stipulation that a licensed adult over the age of twenty-one be in the passenger's seat of the car while the learner is driving.

Mom wasn't about to let her newly minted driver drive her around in her very own car, because, well, Mom is the sensible one in the family, and as any insurance agent can attest, fifteen-year-olds and new cars tend not to play nicely together. Mom also valued her life too much.

In any event, Mom's (well-placed) fears about her new Camry left the task of tutoring a young driver to one Doc Gallagher, he the proud owner of a brand-new, bright red Mercedes sedan.

The first few times driving the Benz were smooth sailing. Not that I had any other cars to compare it to, but the car drove like a dream. (Well, I guess my point of reference was the driver's-ed car—but still.) The suspension was buttery-smooth; and the engine was quiet and powerful. Heads would turn when I drove by. And as a teenager, I noticed.

Those first few trips were, quite literally, the calm before the storm.

A Dark and Stormy Night
The rain was falling in torrents.

You'll forgive my purple prose here that quotes the 1830 novel *Paul Clifford* and its much-maligned opening line. But that's actually what was happening the night of the accident!

It was a Wednesday evening. Not night exactly, but more like late evening. Because of the massive thunderheads, the sky had a sinister, greenish cast. Doc and I were in the Mercedes, and were headed to our church. It's true. My dad is a former pastor; this is where former pastors allow their kids to drive on Wednesday evenings. (Or Sunday mornings, or Sunday nights—we went to church a lot.) In any event, it was dark. Almost. And it was stormy. Lightning illuminated the thick clouds in the distance, and I kicked the windshield wipers up from their auto-sense setting (so cool!) to the constant motion to keep the rain at bay.

About two miles from the church, we arrived at a T intersection that was undergoing some construction work. (I say "some," but it was a lot!) There were some barricades closing off the shoulders of the road going in both directions. Piles of gravel lying beside roadside ditches created to govern water runoff. I remember seeing a bulldozer off to my left as I pulled the car to a stop.

The road at the T intersection was a two-lane access road, meaning that the speed limit for cross traffic was thirty-five miles per hour. So, adhering to the lessons first taught in driver's-ed class, I looked left. Then right. Then left again. I think. And because of the dual challenges that the barricades and the steady rains presented, I began slowly creeping out into the intersection so that I could see; so that I could double-check before pulling out onto the two-lane highway.

I looked both ways that second time. I swear I did. I think. Then I pulled out.

But maybe I looked left, then right, and then forgot to check left again before proceeding. And maybe because it wasn't quite nighttime dark just yet, the oncoming car didn't have its headlights on. Or maybe because this T intersection was on a curve. Or maybe it was because the other car had to have been going at least twenty miles over the speed limit. Or maybe I was distracted by the bulldozer in my line of sight at the moment. Or maybe it was because I was messing with the radio because it seemed like a great time to do it. (Yes, Dad had told me not to mess with the radio and keep my eyes on the road multiple times during this trip that night.)

Whatever it was, the next thing I remember was Dad shouting: "Watch out!"

There was a sickening crunch of metal, and before I realized what had occurred, Dad's Mercedes was now resting at a side-facing angle in the roadside construction ditch.

Thankfully, both Dad and I were OK. In my case, that was owing more to dumb luck than anything else. The front end of the driver's side had absorbed the brunt of the impact, and I could barely get the door open to inspect the damage and check on the other driver involved. Because of the damage to the engine (the entire front was crushed sideways half way through the engine), Dad's brand-new car was now undriveable, but I couldn't help but feel grateful to have exited the car and walked away. The policeman said had the impact occurred just a foot or two further back toward the driver's side door, this might have been a different story. In fact, this might not even be a story that I have lived to tell at all. I felt lucky. And I felt ashamed.

And I felt an overwhelming fear.

In that moment, looking at the crumpled hood of the Mercedes, feeling my legs shake and tremble, I pretty much swore off any notion of getting behind the wheel of a car again.

The driver of the other vehicle was also thankfully unharmed, but the front bumper and hood of her car (a full-sized Buick or Olds if memory serves) were also much worse for the wear. By the time the incident had been through the calculations and inspections of insurance adjusters, my little moment of careless driving had just totaled out two automobiles.

As was the case with me, Dad was able to climb out of the passenger side of the Mercedes, and after also checking to make sure the other driver would not require medical attention, used his cell phone to report the accident to the police. His next call, naturally, was to his wife/my mother Gail, who arrived a few hours later to pick us up in the Camry from where the tow truck towed the car. (I started the evening driving a Mercedes, ended riding in a tow truck—talk about luck!)

The drive home in Mom's car was conducted in almost total silence as had been the past few hours. By the time we had arrived home, Dad had spoken more words to the police and to Gail than to me. In fact, other than asking if I was OK, I don't remember him saying two words to me during the entire episode.

$$\approx$$

To complicate matters, it was finals week at Fort Worth Christian High School. This meant that as soon as we got back home, I grabbed a glass of ice water and headed directly to my room to begin exam prep—reviewing study notes and highlights I had made in my textbooks throughout the semester. This was supposed to be a great week—the last week of school before the summer. Just a few more tough tests to go and I will be free (well, for a few months).

The focus on my studies was a relief; concentrating on schoolwork allowed me to push the images and sounds of the accident into the background. If only for a moment.

After about forty-five minutes of study, I heard the doorknob turn and I looked up from my physics textbook. Dad stood in my doorway. He wore a somber but otherwise unreadable expression. And he said to me only two words:

"Let's go."

I closed by textbook and quietly obeyed the command, rising from my desk. Dad turned and headed downstairs while I slipped on a pair of shoes and walked out of my room, head bowed, feeling like a man being led to his sentencing hearing—or to his execution. To my fifteen-year-old mind, this was it. My moment of reckoning had arrived. Surely I was going to be led into the kitchen, where and Doc and Mom would inform me of the punishment. Were they going to unadopt (is that a thing?) me and send me back to India? Or worse, would the police would be waiting for me at the kitchen table, handcuffs at the ready.

It all made sense now. "Let's go" from my dad really meant, "They're here, the cops, and now you're going to jail for negligent driving."

⁂

But that's not what happened. Instead, Dad was waiting by the front door with Gail's keys to the Camry in his hand. Rather than hand off his son to the authorities, he informed both Gail and me that he needed to retrieve some papers from the Gallagher Financial Group offices for insurance purposes, and since he wouldn't have the Mercedes tomorrow, he needed to go now, and furthermore, that he needed my help since I was the driver.

So, instead of being put into the back of a police cruiser, I was asked to sit in the front seat of a brand-new Toyota. As far as punishments went, helping out on a quick errand for Doc wasn't so bad.

Except that I remember being sure that this was where the silence regarding the accident would finally be broken. I figured that Dad would use the drive over to his office as an opportunity to lecture me about the responsibilities of driving, and about how I needed to pray three times a day thanking God from now until the day I turned sixteen. Or twenty. Or until I died. Three being the number of people I should have injured in the accident. Three being the number of people who walked away unharmed. My dad had grown up Catholic, and I was just waiting for my penance so that I could receive absolution.

But that's not what happened. Instead, Dad pulled the car over to the curb shortly after we had left the house. At the end of our street to be exact. He took a deep breath, stared out at the road ahead, and checked the rear-view mirror for approaching traffic. There was none.

Here it comes, I thought. You know what they say about former preachers and their homilies. Well, actually I don't know what they say, but I thought surely he was getting set to launch into a rather lengthy homiletic story about safety and driving and shepherding through the valley of death's shadow or something. Or have me get out and lay in the road and he was going to run over me a bunch of times. Or…something.

And that's when I received the biggest surprise of that entire evening.

Dad opened the car door, stepped out, and then walked around to the passenger's side while I did nothing but track his movement. He opened the passenger side door. I had not even reached for my seat belt. *What the hell did Dad want?* (I figured it's OK to say "hell" here since I went to church so much as a kid—remember?)

"Drive."

I answered Dad with the sound of my mouth hanging open.

Dad extended his hand and offered me the keys to the car. "Son, please. I want you to get behind the wheel. I want you to drive us to where I tell you to. Let's go!"

Let's go? Me? Wherever he says? Is this what he meant by "Let's go" back at the house? Apparently, it was.

Moving on autopilot, I unbuckled my seat belt and stepped out of the Camry.

Moving on autopilot, I sat down behind the wheel of the Camry and started the car. Remember, this was Mom's *NEW* Camry. Before putting the car in drive, I looked over at Dad. I don't remember asking him a question, but either the expression on my face or the shaking of my hands on the steering wheel must have done the job well enough. What both of those body-language cues were announcing quite loudly was that the last thing I wanted to do that evening was to be behind the wheel. And besides, I had finals that I *had to* study for.

"Son, in life, you're gonna come up on a lot of challenges like this," Dad said. "And when these challenges come up, it's best to face them head on, and right at that moment they crop up." Dad then gestured toward the road out ahead, and concluded with this:

"I know you're scared right now," he said, "but sometimes you have to face the thing you fear the most."

Facing the fear

I'm sure I owe an apology to the people who were behind me that night, because as luck would have it, Dad made me drive a long way. Back toward our church, which was far from where we lived. All the way back to the scene of the accident. If you were one of those drivers, and you wondered why the car in front of you was going twenty-five miles an hour under the speed limit, the answer is this: *I was trying not to get into two wrecks in one evening!* I mean, you've never seen hands on a steering wheel more closely at ten and two in your entire driving life. (I also forgive those of you who flipped me off. Although, maybe it would do us all a little good if we remember that the car in front of us is perhaps being driven by a fifteen-year-old with a learner's permit trying not to total both of his parents' cars in one night. Oh, and learn some manners!)

I also *may* owe an apology to my mom, who was not informed about our excursion in her new Camry. In fairness, a) I didn't know I'd be driving when Dad and I headed out, and b) by the time we got back, I felt like announcing the fact might be a betrayal of some unwritten father-son confidentiality clause.

(And, as I look back on it now, I'm sure Dad *did* tell her, but they just decided to play it as though driving Mom's car without her knowledge was some secret male-bonding rite of passage that could only be shared between fathers and sons. Mom could be sneaky cool like that. Or maybe he didn't tell her because Mom knew me best and may have preemptively called the insurance and filed a claim on the Camry in advance, because after all, I was still a know-it-all teenager.)

In any event, pulling up at that stop sign that very same night was hard to do. No. I'm not phrasing this correctly. I dreaded it. It was downright terrifying to me to drive back to that very same intersection where I had just totaled Dad's new Mercedes, and worse, had almost seriously injured myself and two other people in the process. As we neared the intersection again, the sensation became visceral: knotted stomach, dry mouth, sweaty palms, and elevated heart rate. All of the fight-or-flight things your body does in response to extreme stress or danger were happening all at once. Even writing about it makes my heartbeat race.

Yet, in that moment, I also conquered that fear. I made it to that intersection. Dad and I got out of the Camry, and we stood there for a few moments looking at the tire tracks the Mercedes had left in the roadside ditch. I saw a lot of debris from the accident still scattered across the roadway and the construction site. Dad nodded while we beheld the scene, knowing that no more words needed to be said.

Eventually, Dad simply held out his hand, and I gave him back the keys.

⚬

Facing your financial fears

In that moment behind the wheel of Mom's Camry, a mere hour or two after I caused the accident that totaled Dad's brand-new Mercedes, I was almost overcome with fear over the thought of driving a vehicle. I did not want the risk. The responsibility. The blame that would be heaped upon me if I happened to be involved in another accident.

And then, Dad saved me from that fear. He said, "If you don't face your fear of driving right now, you're going to be afraid of driving for the rest of your life."

So many times in our lives as an investor, saving up for retirement, or deciding on how to allocate our dollars in our budget, or changing how we spend our monthly income, we already *know* the right thing to do.

We're just afraid of it. We have doubts. We're frightened by the prospects of putting an investment vehicle in drive and pushing the gas. *What if the vehicle crashes?* we think. *What if the market crashes? Or what if the market goes up and I miss out on the gains because I was too conservative?* we ask. These fears are reasonable. I had a good reason to be afraid of driving that night. You have good reasons to invest or not to invest in the market. Or to invest in an annuity. Or not to. Or invest elsewhere. Or not.

At the same time, we have these fears of a specific event happening—that's why we need to face these fears head on, and we eventually need to overcome them. Because these reservations can keep us from taking necessary action. And that action may be that you know you need to change financial planners. You know you need to work with an advisor who has your best interests in mind or an advisor with experience or an advisor with credentials such as a CFP®, but you feel stuck. Maybe the person you currently work with is someone you went to high school with, or you know him or her from church, or he or she serviced your parents' accounts way back. In any event, facing your fears and having those tough conversations will only benefit you and your retirement future while avoiding them will only be to your detriment. If you are afraid of change, if you don't like it, join the club. Few do. But remember this, if you don't like change you will like your financial plan being irrelevant a whole lot less.

Because in terms of planning for retirement, as long as our investment vehicles, philosophy, or plans remain stuck in *park*, we will never reach the retirement we're destined for.

5

EATING YOUR FUTURE AWAY

*Only buy something that you'd be perfectly happy
to hold if the market shut down for ten years.*

—Warren Buffett

O ther than the work I did in the offices of the Gallagher Financial Group when I was nine years old, my very first professional experiences in the securities and insurance business began back in October 2006, when I started my own Farmers Insurance and Financial Services business.

For all the funny commercials you see on television, the insurance business can be a cold, ruthless affair, especially for those just starting out in the field. That said, there were some distinct side benefits to underwriting policies, such as the opportunity to study for—and pass, thank you very much—two types of insurance licenses, the series 6, and then the series 63 exams. So, even though my experiences with Farmers were relatively short-lived, the time there did provide me some valuable training.

It also provided me some valuable insight about what works—and especially what doesn't work—when it comes to marketing to potential clients.

As you might guess, keeping a roof over your head as an insurance professional is entirely dependent on either selling new policies, or on renewing existing policies.

Except that new insurance agents don't have many existing polices to renew. Make that exactly no policies. So then, how was a newly minted insurance representative supposed to go out and find new insurance clients?

The answer, according to the advice given at the time, could be found in my oven.

The Land of Milk and Honey. And Cookies.
So, the question put to a young insurance professional: how do you find people who might be interested in buying insurance?

I had no idea. So I asked around. I questioned friends in other walks of life. I sought out the counsel of mentors already in the business. And here's the collective advice I was given by the insurance industry's old guard:

Cookies.

Wait. Cookies, I asked? *What do cookies have to do with the financial business?*

I was told that cookies really aren't the point. The point is that you want to get in good with a lender. Or with a mortgage broker.

And you do that by making the best cookies you can muster.

Because if you bring them cookies, the thinking went, or loaves of pumpkin bread, or can otherwise feed them stuff they love, then they'll naturally repay for their full tummies by sending you a book of business. The realtors will get their home buyers to insure their houses with you; the mortgage brokers will practically sign all the paperwork on your behalf while you're at the beach sipping a drink out of a pineapple.

You just provide delicious baked goods and everything else falls into place.

Since the folks who were giving me this advice seemed like they knew what they were talking about, I took the advice to heart. More to the point, I told Erica about the guidance I'd received, and *she* took that advice to heart. Before long, Erica was spending weeknights hunched over measuring cups and mixing bowls while I was looking up cookie recipes, making trips to the grocery store for supplies (including many gallons of milk), packaging up our "marketing literature," and doing lots of, um..."quality assurance" testing as the cookies emerged from the oven. Yes. Quality assurance. Let's go with that. (I may have also short-cut the process by buying the cookies that you could just throw in the oven and bake. Maybe a few times. Or most. Or all. My memory is a bit foggy.)

All I know is that in terms of business models, it was one of the more *delicious* ones I've encountered, calories be damned. It also got me wondering out loud to Erica whether Famous Amos had begun his cookie empire as a young insurance agent.

(In case *you're* wondering as well, know that Wally Amos, Jr. did *not* work as an insurance agent, but was indeed an agent. Shortly after a stint in the air force, Amos began working for the William Morris Agency in Los Angeles, where he went on to become the firm's very first African-American talent agent. As a talent agent, Amos sent his chocolate-chip cookies to potential clients along with an invitation to visit. He ended up signing many household names using this strategy, including Diana Ross and the Supremes, Sam Cooke, Simon and Garfunkel, and Marvin Gaye. Gaye even loaned Amos $25,000 for Amos to open his first store. So yes. The "send them cookies" sales tactic has been used for decades.)

Armed with a plate stacked with a couple of dozen of Erica's latest culinary creations, I began knocking on doors at mortgage brokers and at realtors, trying to get them interested in my insurance wares. Unfortunately, what I soon discovered was that there was a good reason why all of the insurance professionals had given me the "make them cookies" advice. The gambit was pretty much played out.

I mean, the cookies were a huge hit with the brokers, but they didn't help generate much in the way of new clientele for my Farmers Financial practice. I realized in short order that I needed a new marketing strategy. And actually, the shift in thinking was a welcome one as far as I was concerned. Alas, the cookies that were a hit with the brokers were also beginning to hit my waistline. (And have never left since.)

I did well with Farmers and won a distinguished award that they offer as well as a trip, which was great for a first-year rookie agent, but almost all of those clients came from knocking doors daily in different neighborhoods, introducing myself, and handing them my brochures. It came from walking miles in the one-hundred-plus degree summer and the rainy, icy winter with temperatures in the low teens. It came from dedication and hard work, not from bribes by cookies. By the time I sold my practice with Farmers Financial and started working once more at the Gallagher Financial Group with Dad (as well as working *out* more on the treadmill), the prevailing wisdom about food as a marketing tool had shifted.

It had gone from free desserts to free dinners.

Ugh.

I'm shaking my head as I write this. I should have known better. I did know better. So, it gives me no joy to report that I didn't remember any of the lessons from my year plus trying to get referrals from mortgage brokers and realtors using Erica's restaurant-quality baked goods.

When I began working with Doc again in November 2007, we held several brainstorming sessions about how to go out and "spread the gospel," as it were, about all that GFG could do for a retirement portfolio. We were looking for ways to add to our current marketing efforts, and improve on our existing initiatives. I remember hearing several ideas being bounced around the room. In addition to expanding our reach through the radio (which of course, we ended up pursuing), I recall hearing ideas like magazine advertising, billboards, signage at sports stadiums, television advertising, and sponsorship of charity runs and triathlons. Oh yeah, and hosting fancy dinners—feeding prospective clients *before* giving a brief presentation. (I italicize before because we had been doing dinners for a while but what made us different was that we fed people before the presentation so that they didn't feel like a hostage to our information. We wanted people to stay for the presentation because they valued the material, not because they had to so that they could get a free meal like all of our competitors did. If you didn't want to be there and just wanted a free meal, we didn't want you there. You were free to eat and to leave. That was Doc's way. And it was different. And I think people really appreciated that.)

As with most marketing efforts, we went with a multi-faceted approach. And even though I knew better about one of those facets, I didn't raise my hand and say "hmm...bad idea."

It went exactly as well as I knew it would. But I was the new guy. So, I didn't speak up.

That's why I'm shaking my head.

After about many more years spent touring some of Dallas/Ft. Worth's finest restaurants (well, the ones that could accommodate parties of about fifty), we all but removed ourselves from doing dinners except in rare cases. The demographic of people shifted from those wanting the information to those wanting the meal. And it's hard to blame them. By this time *everyone* was doing free dinners, and they were trained to set their weekly calendars to the postcards that came in the mail. In fact, there were some who most likely went to a different presentation a night from different planners just so that they could eliminate dinners from their budget altogether. And we would have some come to every presentation we had but never come in for a visit.

I came to call this derisively the "bake-sale business." Mind you, I rather enjoyed the work. We ate good meals; we got to educate people about dos and don'ts in their retirement planning. Hey, for an outgoing Texan who's never met a steak dinner he didn't like and who likes to tell a story or two, this was one marketing assignment I didn't mind, and we ended up hosting somewhere between four to eight meet-and-greet dinners every month.

Unfortunately, the hosted dinner/learning sessions just didn't prove a very good investment of *our* time. It became too much of an opportunity cost for Doc and me, even if that opportunity was simply a night spent at home gathered around the dinner table. Those count, too. (In fact, those are the ones I value the most and the only ones that will last for eternity.)

In purely business terms, every evening spent hosting a steak dinner meant an evening not hosting a client meeting or two in our offices. So apart from the occasional special event, the Gallagher Financial Group just doesn't treat people to meals anymore—not at Ruth's Chris, not at Golden Corral, and not even at the Golden Arches.

> *Long term thinking and planning enhances short term decision making. Make sure you have a plan of your life in your hand, and that includes the financial plan and your mission.*

—Manoj Arora, From the Rat Race to Financial Freedom

Look, this is your retirement money we're talking about here. It's certainly not easy to make, and it's not easy to keep, either. But as I pointed out in chapter 1 (and have reiterated in one way or another in subsequent chapters), the pile of money you're working on building and protecting is so much more than that. This is also your life. Your travel. The car you'll drive and the home you'll live in during the twilight of your life. The legacy you'll pass on to your kids, or to charitable organizations.

Yet time and time again, I hear stories in my offices of people make lifelong retirement decisions based on—you guessed it—what they were fed for dinner by some financial planner. (There are some of our competitors who even offer free cookies instead of free dinners at their presentations. Maybe I should have a talk with them and let them know about my experiences and pay it forward, so to speak. On second thought—nah. I'll just let them figure it out.)

Even if you don't choose the Gallagher Financial Group as your independent financial advisor, *please* don't pick a planner based on your appetite. Please. I mean, there's just too much at steak. Wait. I mean, there's too much at *stake*. (See what I did there?)

But all jokes aside, the decision about who to trust with your financial future isn't a decision that should be made between the main course and dessert. Because the wrong advice can mean the difference between spending your retirement greeting new friends as you step aboard a cruise ship and spending your retirement greeting new shoppers as they step through the doors of the store where you work for ten dollars/hour. (And let's face it, at that point, you will need all the free dinners you can get!)

The people trying to get your business may be good at grilling a steak or picking out a wine, but you want them good at picking out *investments*. Or as Doc and I sometimes say on the radio, when it comes to planning for retirement, it's fine to trust your gut, but it's never OK to trust your *stomach*.

So how do you pick?

In chapter 1, I provided some of my background and bona fides when it comes to financial planning. Now, it's time to use that knowledge to help you select a good financial planner, even if that planner doesn't happen to be me.

I'm going to present you with a handy checklist that you can either copy to a notebook or, if you're reading this on an eBook reader, perhaps you can highlight and bookmark for easy reference. What follows is a great list of questions to have ready when you're considering a potential financial advisor for your portfolio:

1. Do you have a Certified Financial Planner™ practitioner working at your firm?
2. How long have you been in business?

3. What are your qualifications?
4. Do you have any referrals I can speak with?
5. Are you a broker, investment advisor, or just an insurance licensed agent? (We'll discuss the differences between the two later in this chapter.)
6. Are you registered with the SEC or FINRA?
7. Do you have a Series 65 license?

The Question Not To Ask

You'll notice that there's nothing on my menu of good questions that involve asking your potential advisor about dinner menus.

Yet here's the thing: our marketing adventures have revealed some very, let's say...*interesting* facets of people's decision-making skills. In fact, as I recall, the GFG has *never* had someone who was planning to attend one of our dinner seminars call the office and ask one of the questions I've just listed. At least not initially.

You know what question we used to get all the time?

What's for dinner?

Unbelievably, it goes even further than that. We've had people call and cancel seminar reservations because they didn't like what was on the evening's menu. Oftentimes, it was because we had selected a restaurant familiar to the prospective attendee, and the prospect wanted a specific menu item instead of the offerings we provided. We've even had people call and try to special order from us or the restaurant. Or get there and order the most expensive thing on the menu and try and add it to our bill. Or try and stick us with a couple of hundred-dollar alcohol tab. (Note to any event planners reading this: to accommodate larger parties, you usually must narrow down a restaurant's menu choices to just two or three menu items. They need to make sure they have enough on hand to serve an extra twenty to forty portions. Also, unless you are OK with buying unlimited drinks or high-priced special orders, make sure and have them take the prospect's credit card at the time of order just as if they were there alone. And reiterate the night of the event to the wait staff all of the above. It will save you a lot of headaches on the back end.)

The other battle we faced, especially more recently, was distraction during the learning session. The cause of this distraction? Anyone with teenagers already knows what I'm going to say: the smartphone.

We found that many attendees would pull out their phones the moment the discussion started and never put it down. They would be on social media or texting friends at the table they had been invited to. A lot would even bring their minor children and talk with them the entire time. It was frustrating. We were asking attendees to be concerned over their financial future; to think about the next thirty or forty years of their lives. And they couldn't focus on the next thirty or forty minutes.

After eating, many seemed more concerned about Facebook than finances.

So, if I've grown to become skeptical about the merits of providing steak dinners, and think that you, too, should share this skepticism when it comes to financial advisors buying you a meal, it does beg the following question. What am I certain about?

Credentials.

Primum non nocere
First, do no harm.

—An excerpt from the Hippocratic Oath.

If you can, help others. If you cannot, do that, at least do no harm to them.

—The fourteenth Dalai Lama,
paraphrasing the Hippocratic Oath.

The Value of Being Certified

As I stated previously in this book, I am a registered investment-advisor representative and a Certified Financial Planner™ practitioner. In layman's terms, I'm certified by the Certified Financial Planning board, and am subject to rules and regulations enforced by the Securities and Exchange Commission—the SEC.

In more technical terms, it means that as a registered investment advisor, I'm governed by a rather dusty law—it's almost eighty years old—called the Investment Advisers Act of 1940, codified at 15 U.S.C. § 80b–1 through 15 U.S.C. § 80b–21. (U.S.C. stands for United States Code. You should probably highlight that entire paragraph as well. Kidding.) The act defines an investment adviser as "any person who, for compensation, engages in the business of advising others, either directly or through publications or writings, as to the value of securities or as to the advisability of investing in, purchasing, or selling securities, or who for compensation and as part of a regular business, issues or promulgates analyses or reports concerning securities." It is enforced and administered by the US Securities and Exchange Commission.

In terms of my status as a Certified Financial Planner™ practitioner, it means that I have passed a comprehensive CFP® Certification Examination; have passed the CFP® Board's Fitness Standards for Candidates and Professionals Eligible for Reinstatement; and have agreed to abide by CFP Board's Code of Ethics and Professional Responsibility and Rules of Conduct, which put clients' interests first. Furthermore, it means that I adhere to the Financial Planning Practice Standards, which spell out what clients should be able to reasonably expect from the financial-planning engagement.

For those of you curious about the full details on all the blood, sweat, and tears behind becoming a Certified Financial Planner™, I invite you to head over to the website www.cfp.net. There, you can learn about the four "*e*'s" of getting an initial CFP® Certification: Education, Examination, Experience, and Ethics. You can also learn that there are only about five thousand Certified Financial Planners in the whole of Texas and only about seventy-seven thousand nation-wide. You will also learn that the CFP® Certification is for financial professionals who are serious and committed to making a career out of providing financial counsel.

In short, it means that I know what I'm doing; that I'm qualified to do what I'm doing; and that I will always carry out my duties ethically and responsibly, putting your best interests ahead of mine.

The Value of Being Certified

Another way of thinking about my financial credentials is this: as a certified and registered investment advisor, I have a *fiduciary duty* to my clients that I will always act in their best interests. Not in my best interests. My clients'. What this means in practical terms is that I must disclose any conflicts of interest. It means my business is conducted "up front" and "in front," as an old baseball coach used to say when discussing reasons why he did or did not play a certain player. *You're out today because you're in a hitting slump,* he might say. Or maybe, *Today, I'm starting you at third base because you've been working hard in practice and have earned a start.* With this particular coach, you always knew where you stood, and for that matter, where he stood. He was an easy coach to play for because of this.

In terms of planning and investing your portfolio, it means that if there is a commission or a fee to the Gallagher Financial Group, I must be completely transparent about the nature of that commission or fee. It means that I'm allowed to make a profit (and, like all businesses, *must* make a profit to stay in business), but I must fully disclose the nature of those profits to you.

The question of fiduciary duty is a very important one for clients to ask of their financial representatives. And get this: it's not a requirement of all those who are involved in the business of picking stocks or funds or other investment vehicles. Brokers are types of financial professionals whose primary obligation is to the firm they work for. You read that right: a broker can put his or her own financial interests ahead of yours. How do I know this? Simple. What happens if that particular broker doesn't meet his or her quota to the firm? Right—he or she would get fired. Doesn't that create a conflict of interest if he or she must sell a certain product to keep up with quota to keep his or her job and you are the next sucker, uh—sorry, person—to walk into his or her office?

Now, in all fairness, sometimes a broker's interests are indeed aligned with an investor's interests. But in most instances, a broker is paid to sell a product. Period.

The other issue is that someone who is only licensed to sell insurance (and not financial investments) can only sell you insurance-based products. So that puts him or her in a bind as far as always being able to always offer you what is in your best interests.

No matter what, all investors should understand this crucial difference between a *broker,* an *insurance only agent,* and a registered investment-advisor representative.

Alas, few do.

The Value of being Independent

I'm about to share a dirty secret of the financial-advising business. Many financial advisors aren't trying to sell you financial counseling. They're trying to sell you specific products. Who offers those products? The companies they represent.

I can't really name names, nor do I really have to.

If you want an everyday comparison, you can think of the independence of our firm the way you think of a travel agent (or the way you think of a travel website like Travelocity, Orbitz, or Booking.com). We can provide the best product and advice, and choose from whatever offers you the best and lowest cost product that matches your objectives. For example, if you call up Delta Airline's 1-800 number, you're going to get prices and options only for Delta flights. But if you call up a travel agent (or click over to Travelocity), you're going to get prices for flights from Delta, United, Southwest, and so on. Just like a travel agent will find you the lowest cost and most efficient way to get you from point A to point B, the Gallagher financial Group is going to recommend the most efficient way to get from starting point A to financial goal B, regardless of the vendor.

Why? We're *independent*.

And in terms of names, the name I will mention is the Gallagher Financial Group, and I mention it because we are not tied to a specific brokerage house. We do not have sales quotas to meet. If we don't meet a quota for a specific company's products, we're not going to get fired by the company creating, marketing, and selling those products.

Some final thoughts about meal planning

As you've seen in this chapter, there are some very important pieces of data you should have about your financial advisor before committing any of your hard-earned dollars to his or her care. Fortunately, this information is relatively easy to find out. In most cases, all you have to do is ask.

Unfortunately, not many investors are prepared with the sorts of questions I've presented earlier. And Doc even has his own "best question to ask your financial planner," which he believes is even better than those: *If I didn't have any money with you, would you still care about me.* The answer to that question (often through their expression, seldom verbal) will show you if that financial professional looks upon you as a person of God-given worth or as an item of profit. We were meant to value people and use things not use people and value things. Sadly, many in this business have forgotten that. And it's a shame that many prospective clients don't know to search out answers to these important questions. (Unfortunately, not all investors have read this book.)

Remember, many investors get into trouble because they choose advisors because they are friends at church. Or because they coach their kid's pee-wee soccer team. Or because they've recently reconnected on Facebook. Make no mistake, though, you can get terrible financial advice from a very nice man or woman. Nice is only a small part of the equation for picking the right advisor.

Even more unfortunately, many investors will base decisions that affect their financial futures using the worst possible rationale of all: what the advisor fed them for dinner on some random Tuesday or Thursday evening.

Don't let that be you. Make a wise financial decision, and look for a Certified Financial Planner™ practitioner like myself. Look for a registered investment-advisor representative. Because with a solid financial plan working on your behalf, you won't be dependent on someone else's marketing efforts to eat that filet mignon.

With the right financial advice, you can go out and treat *yourself* to a great dinner just about any time you please. And you won't have to listen to a presentation to get it!

6

THE ANGRY BIRD CATCHES THE WORM

*Investing should be more like watching paint
dry or watching grass grow. If you want
excitement, take $800 and go to Las Vegas.*

—*Paul Samuelson*

A little while back, I took Jaden to a matinee. It was time to give Erica a break, so it was an official boy's afternoon out. The choices on that day were something with explosions, an R-rated comedy, *Angry Birds*, and something else with explosions and a serial killer or something. In other words, for a father taking his six-year-old son to the movies, there was *Angry Birds*…or there was *Angry Birds*. (Also, the R-rated comedy was sold out. *Kidding*! They only had one seat and there were two of us. Again, *Kidding*! Please don't write me letters about how you didn't like this joke—I won't read them.)

We saw *Angry Birds*. Jaden had a blast. And while I didn't dream I'd get much enjoyment out of a movie featuring characters from a phone video game, whose job in said game is to fly through the air and then…something, I had a pretty good time as well. This despite the fact that *The Angry Birds Movie* contained more than its share of a few jokes aimed squarely at the adults accompanying their kids in the theater. Who knows, maybe that stuff is in the game too. (I confess I haven't played it. In a while.) I'll take a Pixar animated movie any day of the week, though.

Movie reviews aside, Jaden and I enjoyed our hanging-out time—eating popcorn, Junior Mints, and Reese's Pieces, and otherwise ruining our dinner. But that's what guy days are all about, I suppose. During the car ride home, we both took turns discussing our favorite scenes. As with all such outings, it was less about the activity, and more about the *time.*

About a week afterward, I was out again, this time on a quick shopping errand to Wal-Mart. When I arrived at the end of one of the aisles, I saw a big end-cap display of Angry Birds merchandise. (Note to self: I'm in the wrong business. I should be designing games, selling off the toy licensing rights, and then depositing piles of cash in my bank account every Friday afternoon. Have you seen the price tag on an Angry Birds stuffed animal?) I immediately grabbed a bright red bird that was situated on a shelf directly in my line of sight and thought of how Jaden would love it. But I didn't want my three-year-old, Jensen, to feel left out so I bought him a character too even though he hadn't seen the movie yet. The people marketing at Wal-Mart are nobody's fool; they know exactly how tall most of their target shoppers will be. Even if those target shoppers are dads and not always kids.

So naturally, being the father of the year candidate that I am, I put up no resistance whatsoever to the inner voice that told me that Erica would say the kids have plenty of toys. And I mean plenty. I tend to be a shopaholic when it comes to our boys, and we have a toy closet of stuff they haven't even received yet that we are saving for special occasions. And someone keeps adding to it. (*Cough—as I look in the mirror.) I'm soon headed to the checkout counter with the cart full of the household necessities I've come for, plus *four* brand-new *talking* Angry Birds stuffed animals.

You read that correctly: The Angry Birds stuffed animals speak when squeezed. They are capable of repeating several phrases per animal, but the phrase that sticks in my memory is one from the pig character that I gave Jensen:

"Come on, Leonard."

The backstory: apparently, whatever Angry Birds character this toy is a replica of (he's nameless, if memory serves) has a fellow Angry Bird pig whose name is Leonard, and Leonard is in frequent need of annoyed reminders. Again, I'm hardly an expert on games featuring pigs under attack from exploding fowl.

In any event, the reason this phrase sticks out so clearly, not only for myself, but now for our entire family, is because the phrase "Come on, Leonard," when filtered through the ears of my three-year-old, became this phrase instead:

"Come on, *Lizard*."

It was one of those moments that was probably much funnier hearing it than reading it on a page. And it kind of reminds me of another movie, this one an all-time classic: *Bull Durham*. It reminds me of the scene on the bus where Kevin Costner's Crash Davis corrects Tim Robbins's Nuke LaLoosh when he keeps singing the wrong lyrics of a song. "Nobody's got *stress*," Crash tells Nuke. "They're wearing a *dress*."

In *Bull Durham*, Crash gets exasperated at Nuke for messing up the lyrics to an Otis Redding tune. However, in the case of Jensen's misunderstanding of his toy bird, the turn of phrase was endearing. Thus, the phrase "Come on, Lizard" quickly found its way into the Gallagher household vocabulary.

It also got me thinking about financial planning.

☙

Hey, thinking about financial planning is what I do. Don't judge. After doing this for over twenty years, I can't just stop my brain from mulling over people's retirement plans any more than the poor, poor pigs of Bird Island can't stop their city from being target practice for fat, red (and various other colored), grumpy parakeets.

(Edit: Jaden has entered the room while I was typing up this last sentence. He asked what I was working on, and so I brought him up to speed my recollections about *Angry Birds*. He informed me that I had it all wrong: that Leonard was the King of the green pigs, and therefore no friend to Chuck the Bird, and that the pigs tricked the birds to take over their home, forcing the birds to take back the island from the invading green pig horde. So, there's that. And speaking of brains, Jaden also thinks that I may be suffering from some sort of acute brain injury for not being able to instantly recall all things *Angry Birds Movie* the way he can. My response is to point out the irony in telling a story about a child getting something wrong about *Angry Birds*, when in fact the adult is getting several things wrong. Jaden's response is to look at me like I'm the world's biggest idiot for trying to explain irony to a six-year-old. World without end.)

Leonard vs. Lizard. When Misunderstandings are Costly
As mentioned, my wife Erica and I eventually started incorporating "Come on Lizard" into the linguistic shorthand that's unique to our family. I'm sure you know what I'm talking about—I'm sure you use phrases or nicknames that wouldn't make a lick of sense to anyone unfamiliar with the inner workings of your family.

In our case, "Come on, Lizard" is becoming a Gallagher inside joke that can be deployed as a stand-in for almost *any* misunderstood conversation or sentence. "Lizard" is even becoming something of a nickname for Jensen. Whenever I need him to follow me somewhere, I can just say "Come On, Lizard!" and he'll laugh and say it back as he follows.

Misunderstandings by a three-year-old are a shared experience for us all. They are cute. They are frequently hilarious. And most of all, they are harmless because they often involve fuzzy stuffed animals based on movie characters.

But when your retirement hangs in the balance, misunderstandings between financial advisors have much more dire consequences. These types of misunderstandings aren't the ones we chuckle about over the dinner table. They are the ones that can cause us heartache, and in some cases, can even affect our day-to-day schedules. In other words, these aren't the kind of misunderstands we can afford.

Fortunately, I have a few excellent tools at my disposal to make sure that "Come on Lizard"—type misunderstandings only apply to your kids or grandkids, and never to your retirement accounts.

⁑

Tool One. The interview.
When potential clients visit my office at the Gallagher Financial Group for the very first time, I always start with an interview.

Which reminds me—have I mentioned that I'm in the relationship business? And that the relationships are built on a foundation of trust and understanding? Only about a dozen times by now, right? The point is this: the interview is the inflection point for that relationship; it's where that relationship formally begins. If people don't appreciate the many questions that I am asking and just tell me to stick to the one account they came in for, I politely end the interview and ask them to leave. What I do is all about a holistic approach, and I believe that not any one asset or investment is a stand-alone account. Each one affects the other in one way or another whether the client or prospect realizes it or not. So, it's important for me to make sure I understand all the forces at play before I can address any single pressing issue.

While it certainly isn't a job interview, nor a *60 Minutes* interview, the questions new prospects can expect from me are thorough. They may even take you a bit outside your comfort zone. It's understandable. Generally speaking, people are very private when it comes to their finances. But I ask a broad-ranging set of questions, not because I want to see you squirm in our chair, but because the nature of my job *demands* that I fully develop a picture of your finances and fiscal objectives. If I didn't ask, I wouldn't be doing my job. I need to know where you stand, and I need to know where you'd like to journey to. So how do I do that?

I usually start by gathering many of the facts that appear on pieces of paper. I do this because, to give you *good* advice, I need to know about the *numbers* associated with your financial life: what your 401(k) looks like, whether or not you have an annuity, a pension, social security benefits, CDs, real-estate holdings, and so on. The financial picture that needs to be painted is meticulous. We dig down into the nitty-gritty, down to the balances in your savings and checking accounts.

But eventually, the interview turns to questions of a more personal nature. And we do this not because I'm nosy, but because I need to know who you are as a person, in order to give you *exceptional* advice.

I need to know, for example, if you are caring for a special-needs child or a parent suffering the effects of Alzheimer's. I need to know if you expect to retire at age sixty or seventy-two, or if you can't imagine a retirement that doesn't include the satisfaction of still reporting to work thirty hours a week. And I should know about that particular life goal. My dad, Doc, has tried to enjoy his goals of slowing down for retirement, only to discover that retirement doesn't seem to give him much joy. He's not a huge fan of golf; however, he *is* a huge fan of the work he does. At this stage of his life, he treats his work more like a calling than a profession. So, more power to him, I say. (In fact, I can say it most days by just shouting down the hallway.)

In short, I need to know about parts of your life that won't necessarily show up on the bottom line of an account statement.

I'm in the relationship business. And the interview is where you and I begin that relationship. And as with many relationships, one of the first things I'm looking for is whether or not there's a *match*. I'll explain.

Match the Numbers With the Personal

The entire reason I'm writing this chapter right now is because of what I discover so many times as I conduct these first-time interviews with potential clients. As you might imagine, sometimes it takes several days for me to gather all the numbers associated with a new client's financial life. And by the time I do get those numbers, and then compare the figures against what the prospect told me about his or her goals and desires during our initial interview, I encounter this revelation that shouldn't surprise me after all these years, but always does.

It's this: The numbers and the objectives don't match.

In other words, the products these prospects are often invested in don't have a counterpart with the financial objectives expressed during the interview.

Sometimes, I'll see three or four financial goals being expressed, but the goals are completely incongruent with one another. I've encountered retirees who express safety as their main objective, yet have a margin account open at a brokerage (yes, I said margin). Other examples include investors looking for long-term growth whose IRA is 80 percent allocated in a government bond fund.

In each of these cases where objectives do not align with investment vehicles, the root cause usually comes down to a simple misunderstanding. These investors thought they were advancing a retirement that said "Leonard."

Instead, they had authorized the purchase of retirement products that screamed out "Lizard."

Your job is to know which is which.

My job is to clearly communicate the difference. My job, you might say, is to make sure you know the red birds from the green pigs.

Not Happy Clients. *Enthusiastic* Clients

When you sit down to speak with your financial advisor, whomever that might be, make sure that there is an actual conversation happening, and not just two people talking at each other. I've had more than

MATTHEW GALLAGHER WITH BRIAN CULP

a few new clients relay feelings that their previous advisor seemed like they were just waiting for their turn to talk, rather than actively listening to their clients.

And remember that as with all conversations, it's an exercise that requires both parties to participate. If you hear an idea thrown out by a financial advisor, make sure that idea matches (there's that word again) with the objectives laid out earlier in the conversation. Ultimately, you are the one who bears ultimate responsibility over your retirement plans. Not your friend, not your neighbor, and not even your financial planner.

So, make sure to participate in the discussion. As a result of your conversation with me, not only will you be happy about the plan that has been set in motion, but you'll also be able to articulate that plan—and the rationale *behind* your plan—to your buddies on the golf course. Or your neighbors in the front yard. Or during movies like *Angry Birds*. Wait. Strike that last one.

Conversations in movie theaters: bad.

Conversations while you're speaking to your financial advisor: beyond good.

Because of those real conversations the Gallagher Financial Group has each and every day with new customers and old, we not only create happy clients, as Doc would say, but we create enthusiastic clients.

The Impact of Conversations

I remember very clearly one client in particular who ended up choosing the Gallagher Financial Group after several of those conversations I just referenced. His name was Allen (although I've changed his name for the sake of privacy), and he had a round face and warm blue eyes that smiled along with the rest of him, especially when he was looking at his wife, watching and listening as she answered some of my questions.

When he decided to move their portfolios over to the care of our office, he called me privately right after they left and told me this:

"The reason I chose you over other financial advisors, Matthew, is because my wife felt comfortable with you. She said you were the only one who truly sought out her input and listened to her concerns. And I'm confident that if anything were to ever happen to me and I wasn't here one day, I know that you would take good care of her."

I thanked Allen for the kind words, and welcomed both him and his wife (I'll call her Grace) into the GFG family. Neither of us realized how true those words would become.

Just a handful of weeks after opening their accounts, Allen called me with terrible news. He had been diagnosed with pancreatic cancer (I've changed the exact condition as well). He thought that with proper treatment he could still live a long but debilitated life. Unfortunately, that wasn't in God's plans. I remember coming in to work a number of months later and hearing that Grace had called for me multiple times that morning. I somberly returned the call because I just knew what she was going to say. I was right. Allen had passed away.

Since that phone call, I've worked with Grace on numerous occasions. She remains a client to this day. As always, our work together begins in the same way it always has: with a conversation. A conversation about the client and what he or she wants and needs out of life.

The conversations are almost never about money.

Conclusion

Whether we recognize it or not, personal finances affect us all—young and old, healthy or infirmed. So, too, can misunderstandings about those finances. So many times when I've asked clients why they were invested a certain way they've replied saying they didn't know. They didn't understand what the planner was saying or how what he or she suggested was going to help. And too many times they didn't ask either. They just smiled and shrugged and nodded. They allowed "lizard" to replace "Leonard" in their financial hopes and dreams. They looked upon that planner the way we look at Jensen when he misunderstands. The difference is their planner isn't three and their financial hopes and dreams being forever changed isn't cute.

When Jensen first got the new Angry Bird's pig and then misquoted the toy, Erica and I smiled and nodded and played along. We patted Jensen on the head and sent him to the room where the pig could join the other stuffed animals in our sons' bed.

Just like, as we draw this chapter to a close, I want to reiterate the point: when it's coming from the mouth of a three-year-old, misunderstandings are perfectly fine! They're adorable, in fact. They'll become part of the fabric of your family history.

But if you ever misunderstand something a financial advisor is telling you, nodding along and smiling is most certainly *not* the way to go. You are not three. Neither is the advisor you're considering hiring. It is not adorable or cute to sign up for something that will not act according to your financial desires. And should that misunderstanding result in a financial misstep, it could very well rip the fabric of your family savings. And you will have *no one* to blame but yourself!

7

THE HOCKEY DILEMMA

When we live in the present, we are alert to what's
actually happening—to us and in the world at large,
we can then act based on that awareness. And financial
planning based on reality tends to lead to better results...
When we live in the future, we are lost in fantasy or
fear. When we live in the past, we are lost in regret or
nostalgia. Financial planning based on fantasy, fear,
regret, and nostalgia is likely to lead to more of the same.

—Carl Richards, *The Behavior Gap: Simple*
Ways to Stop Doing Dumb Things with Money

This chapter begins with a story from the Gallagher chronicles that involves an act of balancing. Specifically, it involves gliding around a sheet of ice while balanced on a steel blade approximately one-eighth of an inch wide. This while trying to keep control of a little rubber disk and hitting at the rubber disk with a thin, crooked stick. For those of you who have been on ice skates, you know that when just starting out, this is no small feat. It's often a process of falling on your face a few times before finding an equilibrium that works for you.

In the latter parts of the chapter, I segue into a discussion of balance when it comes to retirement planning. It too can be a process of finding an equilibrium that works; that keeps you gliding forward with grace, rather than spinning headlong into the unknown.

So, let's lace up our investing skates and jump right in.

To Skate. Or Not to Skate.

When he was just three years old, we got Jaden enrolled in ice hockey. It's true: in the Dallas/Ft. Worth area, the land of 105-degree summers, there are actually sheets of ice open year-round where kids and adults alike can skate for fun, or at the very least skate for the thrill of hitting a hockey puck into the back of a net.

(To support Jaden's hockey pursuits, I also enrolled in hockey a few years later. To my great shame, there is video proof of this, which is considered highly classified Gallagher intel. The video is shared only with clients, and even then, only with clients who I'm sure will laugh with me and not at me when watching me play hockey.)

Granted, age three is a young age to be thinking of playing hockey. But that really wasn't our goal. Erica and I had more general plans. Through skating and hockey, Jaden would begin learning about teamwork. Because he was doing something difficult, he'd see himself mastering that challenge, and thus begin developing self-confidence. In addition, we hoped that the time on skates would give him further options athletically as he continued to grow and develop, as the coordination, strength, and balance needed to keep upright on a pair of skates would be of use in almost any other athletic endeavor.

But most of all, we just wanted him to have a blast.

On that count, he most definitely surpassed expectations. It wasn't that he enjoyed hockey—it was that he couldn't wipe the smile off his face each time he came off the ice and changed back into tennis shoes.

In fact, all of what I've just described is exactly the reasoning given by the USA Hockey website about reasons to start your kid in hockey, and start them out young. (Small plug for USA Hockey ahead.) Maybe that's why youth-hockey participation is at an all-time high. According to the USA Hockey website, there were a record 115,694 participants enrolled at the eight-and-under level for the 2016–17 season. This is the highest participation level in USA Hockey's eighty-year history. This statistic includes a record number of *first-year* participants in the under-eight category, a record number of *returning* U8 participants, and a record number of *female* U8 players. If youth hockey were tracked the same way that stock markets are tracked, the indexes would be sitting at historic highs.

So, look out, Canada: the Gallagher boys and just over one hundred thousand of their on-ice colleagues have figured out how much fun hockey is, and are now gunning for your national pastime.

Now, when three-year-olds start playing hockey, they don't even dress up in full pads. There are a few skating sessions prior to putting on the shoulder pads, elbow pads, and shin guards, helmet, and all the other pads that follow. If you can't skate over to the puck, after all, then there's no use having a stick in your hands.

It was during this first full-pad session when Jaden's love of skating around became a full-fledged *looove* of hockey, on par with the *loooove* of his Thomas the Train piggy bank (discussed back in chapter 2). In fact, he loved his first full hockey practice so much that he came off the ice that afternoon with the announcement that serves as the theme of this chapter.

Erica and I were both there watching the first practice. The coach huddled up the roughly twenty-five exhausted and excited skaters—excuse me, hockey players. He told them all that it was a great job, and then dismissed them for the day. Jaden skated directly over to us, and Erica unsnapped his helmet while I shot a few proud dad pics with my iPhone.

"How was practice, Jaden?" Erica asked. "Did you just have so much fun out there?"

Jaden took a deep breath so that he could reply. He was still catching his breath after almost an hour of skating at top speed. But the excitement in his eyes lit up the entire rink.

"Mom! I don't want to tell people about Jesus anymore when I grow up," Jaden announced loudly. "I want to be a hockey player!"

※

I was taken aback. My finger hovered over the camera button on my iPhone (I guess it's a button for other things as well) while I stammered for the right words.

As is her habit, Erica had all the right answers. After a quick blush passed across her cheeks, Erica gave Jaden a warm smile. She knelt to Jaden's eye level and placed a reassuring arm on our son's padded shoulder. She lowered her voice, responding with a calm enthusiasm of her own. "Honey, you can do *both*," she said, her eyes radiating warmth and kindness. "You can play hockey and still do other things. You can play hockey and tell people about Jesus. Most things in life don't have to be one or the other. Isn't that great?"

Jaden nodded, more excited than he was before his announcement. I could see from his expression that he had just decided to become the NHL's first ordained minister who could also compete for the Conn Smythe trophy.

(The Conn Smythe, for those of you not raised in colder climates, is the award given to the player who is the most valuable in the NHL play-offs. The current holder is Pittsburgh Penguins star Captain Sydney Crosby who has won back-to-back trophies, and back-to-back Stanley Cups, by the way. Why did you think I was talking about the MVP in the entire NHL? That award would be the Hart Trophy. I mean, come on. Everybody knows that. Well, everybody who was raised on a steady diet of Dallas Stars games every October through April—and sometimes into June back when they were good and went deep into the play-offs yearly!)

In any event, it was a cute moment between mother and son, and obviously, a moment that's become etched in memory. It was a thrill for a dad to watch his child thrill to a new activity; to watch the exuberance and innocence expressed by a wide-eyed, churchgoing five-year-old after his first-ever, full-pads hockey practice.

What's more, Erica's discussion about Jaden's professional-hockey prospects set me to pondering over a question the rest of that day:

You know what else doesn't have to be one or the other?

You already know what I'm going to say.

Your Money. It Can Do Two Things At Once.
As you have learned in previous chapters, most of my work in financial planning involves building relationships with new clients, while also enhancing relationships with existing clients. How do I do that? By having conversations. Lots of them. Hundreds every month, and thousands every year.

When it comes to these retirement-planning conversations, many of the people I talk to tend to fall into one of two different camps, and the two camps are at philosophical odds with one another.

One of these camps I'll call the "safety" camp.

The other I'll call the "stock-market" camp.

The convictions of the folks in each of these camps can take on almost political overtones. And I don't mean that in a good way. The two camps can become as polarized as the political camps in our current political climate. Well, almost. Nothing's quite *that* bad.

But generally speaking, the people who fall into each of these two camps view the *other side* as 100 percent wrong, 100 percent of the time.

And folks who hold one of these two world views are just…wrong.

For example, when I visit with the "safety" investors about the stock market, the refrain I hear time and again goes like this: "The stock market is bad. Practically a casino, and just like all casinos, it's rigged in favor of the 'house.'" The stock market was bad yesterday. Trying to invest in stocks is a fool's errand today, and even if things are going up for now, as sure as the sun rises in the East, it will not end well. Therefore, we need to look for any investments other than the stock market. Mattresses, coffee cans, heck even Bitcoin—anything is better than trying to pick stocks."

Meanwhile, the "stock-market" investors take the opposite approach. Here's a typical argument I get from someone 100 percent in the stock-market camp:

"The stock market is good. Because the stock market always goes up. Sure, there might be a hiccup here and there, but no one ever lost money in the stock market over time unless he or she were really stupid about it. So just set it and forget it. Safety is for suckers who don't like getting 10–12 percent on their money year after year. Annuities, bonds, CDs, T-bills, precious metals? Pffft. All of these are just ways to guarantee underperforming the market, and thus guarantee that you'll be waiting longer and working harder to retire."

So, which of these camps most describes your outlook on investing? And more significantly, which of these two camps is *correct*?

Well, the answer to that is similar to most questions when discussing political matters. Sure, it's more fun to yell and gnash our teeth and think of creative ways to insult the opposing "team," but both camps share a common goal. Growing wealth and protecting wealth.

In reality, the *best* approach requires that we find some middle ground.

Or, to use the illustration that kicked off this chapter: just like my son coming off the ice and thinking that he had to shove aside the Gospels in favor of his pursuit of NHL stardom—that you can live and breathe the Bible or the Stanley Cup, but not both—there is a third option worth considering.

In other words, the answer to the "safety" versus "stock market" question is this:

"Yes."

And unlike so much else in the financial-planning business, this is one answer I can be certain of.

A Man of Unshakable Certainty

Let's talk about that old stock market of ours for a sentence or two. (And by old, I do mean *old*. US citizens have been trading stocks of US-based companies, including Alexander Hamilton's First Bank of the United States, since the 1790s.)

I have one prediction when it comes to investing in the stock market: I have no idea what will happen in the stock market. I don't know what will happen tomorrow. I don't know what will happen next month or next year. I don't know what the Fed will do about interest rates. Beyond a general range, I don't know what the rate of inflation will be. I don't know what will happen to large cap stocks, or small cap, or sector-based ETFs, or mutual funds tied to the energy arena, or to real estate. None of it.

We're clear on this point, yes? *I have no clue* what's going to happen with the US stock market in the future.

Oh, and I have one other prediction when it comes to the stock market: I'm positive where the stock market will go in the years ahead. They say that there are only two certainties in life: death and taxes. To that, I'd like to add a third: the US stock market will increase in value.

But how can I make this prediction? How can I be so certain about the future of the stock market when I've spent time in previous chapters telling you that it's wise to protect yourself against a possible stock-market crash?

Because it *is* wise.

Because the stock market will go up. And the stock market will also correct.

That's why you need balance.

What Works in Hockey Works in the Market.

So, let's spend a brief section discussing the downsides of investing in the stock market. Downsides in the stock market go by one of two names: *corrections* and *bear markets.*

A stock-market correction is a loss of 10 percent in the value of the overall market. For example, a market that goes from one thousand to nine hundred has just *corrected.* Sometime in the future, the stock market will correct. It's just a matter of time.

Bear markets are corrections with, uh…claws. A bear market is a loss of 20 percent. The market that goes from one thousand to eight hundred has just entered bear-market territory. Sometime in the future, the stock market will enter a bear market. Again, it's just a matter of time.

How can I be so certain, even though I'm not in the prediction business? Well, since 1900, there have been 123 corrections of the US stock market. That's a rate of roughly one correction per year. One correction per year whether your hockey team won the Stanley Cup or didn't make the play-offs. One per year whether you loved or hated the president, the size of the national debt, the state of Social Security, the top marginal tax rate, the chairman of the Fed, or heck, even the House Minority Whip. (In fact, I take this as some small comfort. Our country and our economy are so much bigger than one election, one news event, or one man or woman. And no, I can't name the House Minority Whip off the top of my head.)

So again, the stock market will fall. Even when it's rising, it falls. We've been on an extended bull market starting in 2009, and it's still going strong at the time of this writing.

And still, according to stats compiled by Yardini Research, the market dropped 19.4 percent in 2011 (just missing the official 20 percent threshold to call it a bear market). In 2015, it dropped 12.4 percent over a ninety-six-day period. In late 2015 and 2016, it dropped 13.3 percent over a one hundred-day period.

Heck, back in 2010, the Dow dropped almost one thousand points, or 9.2 percent, before recovering almost all that loss. In one afternoon. Less than that, in fact. The whole thing took about forty-five minutes. You could have been at a dentist appointment while the "Flash Crash" was going on during the afternoon of May 6, 2010, when the market went into correction territory and was back out again. The only way you could have predicted that one was by inventing a time machine sometime in 2009. (And if that happened, no one's told me about it.)

Hockey players fall. They get up. This is how it works.
Of course, we remember bear markets more acutely than corrections, because when bear markets are happening, most of the investing public thinks that the world is going to end. I'm here to tell you it doesn't.

The US stock market during the recovery from 2009 to 2015 increased nearly 200 percent. Want to reverse time just a little bit further? The bear market of 2002 had several causes, but the most prominent were linked to the bursting of the dot-com bubble in 2000, followed by the terror attacks of September 11, 2001. However from NASDAQ's close at a five year low in June 2002, the S&P 500 and Dow closed higher and the NASDAQ posted the best first half since 2009 in June 2017.

Over its modern history (since 1900), this is the way the market works.

What I'm saying is that the best place to invest your money and watch it grow is the stock market. *At the same time,* what I'm saying is that the next *correction* to that amazing wealth engine is coming, as sure as night follows day. I'm also saying that the next *bear market* is coming as well.

Over its modern history (since 1900), this is the way the market works.

And although I don't have a crystal ball, I can *almost guarantee* that the causes of the next bear market won't have anything to do with the previous bear market. House loans are considerably harder to get today than they were during the housing market run-up of 2005–2008.

In looking at the dot-com bubble, my opinion is that this has largely been dealt with as well. In 2000, the Internet was still a very new thing in the commercial and business world, and poorly understood as a result. Companies like AOL were sporting trailing P/E ratios of 100, and they were hardly the only such company with very expensive valuations. (Imagine if Ford started selling pickup trucks not for $50,000 but for $500,000 and you have some idea about how out of whack prices were getting at the time.)

But eventually people realize that companies need to sell things and generate cash and profit no matter whether they're newfangled dot-coms or not. So, contrast the AOL situation in 2000 with that of Apple, which is now the world's most valuable company. (Google is a close second and on some days has even surpassed Apple.) Another bubble looming? Again, I can't make promises, but the numbers don't suggest it. Apple has a trailing P/E of 10. They are sitting on a $200 billion pile of cash. They pay out the highest dividend (measured in dollars) of any company on the planet.

Investing is a simple process of taking into account the present value and future value. The other major factor to understand here, is what you lose as a result of inaction. Consider what you can gain and what you can lose in your decision.

—J. R. Rim

Keep Your Balance.

What I'm saying is that in order to be prepared for your retirement years, you should understand that the stock market will go up and it will go down. So basically, I'm saying you should participate in the upside of the market, and protect yourself from the downside.

What I'm saying is that the answer to "stock market" versus "safety" is "it depends."

And I'm also saying that you need to see a balance in your investment portfolio.

And most importantly, what I'm saying is that you should work with a Certified Financial Planner™ practitioner like myself to find a middle ground that's based on your personal financial situation.

Because in your personal financial situation, having 60 percent of your portfolio invested in an annuity might be a perfect balance for you. Conversely, your balance might mean that 80 percent of your portfolio is in market-based mutual funds or ETFs.

What's important is that you should have that conversation with your financial planner, and find the balance that's most suited to your goals, needs, and your personality.

A final note about that last point, which I'll use to close the chapter: they say that great skaters in hockey are the ones who can "feel" the ice through their skate blades. In fact, hockey players have several techniques for obtaining this feel. For example, there are a wide variety of blade types, all with differing characteristics. Some blades are built for greater acceleration, some for greater turning, and so on. Some hockey players don't wear socks when skating—they believe bare feet *feel* the ice better than feet covered by cotton. Believe it or not, some players even *bake* their skates—like cookies in the oven—to get them to mold to their feet more closely!

No two combinations of these factors are *perfect* for every skater. What works for Sidney Crosby might be different from what works for Alex Ovechkin, which might be different from what works for...Jaden Gallagher (fingers crossed).

So, too, it is with retirement planning. A mix of investment products and investment styles are indeed appropriate for almost every portfolio. Generally speaking, a healthy retirement is fueled by a balance of stocks, ETFs, or mutual funds, annuities or other alternative investments, and possibly even a mix of bonds or real estate (and just a little in cash).

However, finding the combination that molds to your personality and comfort level is the key. A perfect pair of skates won't help much if they hurt your feet the entire time you are skating and leave you feeling uneasy on the ice. And a *perfect* investment allocation won't help much if it leaves you feeling anxious and uneasy about your chances for enough growth to retire on and a reliable income after retirement.

8

HOW TO STAY ALIVE DURING A BREAK-IN

*Doing your own financial planning is like
doing your own appendectomy...*

—Doc Gallagher

This chapter features a retelling of an event that I can laugh about now. Kind of.

Which reminds me: you might have noticed something about stories the people tell about "things they can laugh about today." At the time when these events were happening, they are anything but hilarious. "Things we can laugh about now" are usually an account of some of life's most terrifying moments.

That's certainly the case here.

🦢

When Jaden Getting Ready Isn't All It Seems.
It was a Friday morning. Late springtime. 2015. I was running late to the office for reasons I can't quite remember; the reason I can't recall little details like these will become clear momentarily.

Anyway, it's getting close to nine o'clock in the morning, and I still need to jump in the shower. Erica is up and generally preparing for the day. An important and necessary aside about the physical geometry of the Gallagher house, by the way: We live in a two-story house, and like many such houses, the bedrooms are upstairs. The kitchen, living room, family room, and so on are downstairs. And the southern wall of the family room is a sliding glass door that opens to our ground-level covered patio.

So, Erica is upstairs. Somewhere. The kids are also upstairs each in their separate rooms. As mentioned, I'm in the master bedroom and just about to jump into the shower. In the bedroom closest to ours, one-year-old (at the time) Jensen is sleeping soundly. In the bedroom next to that, I can hear our four-year-old (at that time) Jaden rummaging around. Loudly. Banging on the walls like drums as was his habit. And still is. Or at least that's what I thought. I didn't pay much attention to the banging, as there's certainly nothing unusual about Jaden making a bit of noise in the morning. The child often wakes sometime between eight and nine o'clock and immediately heads over to his closet to pick out clothes for the day, or what toys to play with, or sometimes—to judge from the clunking and thunking Erica and I hear coming from Jaden's room—working on some kind of house addition. I should mention here that Erica is a retired eleven-year public-school teacher who now stays home with our boys and homeschools them, so there isn't a rush by them to get out of the door to catch the bus. In fact, at that time they always did school at the kitchen table, which was just a few feet from the sliding glass door that opens to the kitchen dining area.

The banging that morning was getting so loud that I was about to make a small detour down the hallway so that I could tell Jaden to stop making so much noise, or else he'll wake his brother (sounds familiar, parents?). But I decided that I didn't even have time for that. And thus, I'm dressed only in a pair of red gym shorts, striding toward the bathroom to jump into the shower, when the next banging I hear is much more distinct: it's coming from our master bathroom door.

The thumping this time is from Erica, and while she's slamming her fist on the door, she's shouting words that no one wants to hear.

"MATTHEW! SOMEONE IS TRYING TO BREAK IN!!"

In my memories of this event, I can still hear the piercing, electric undercurrent of panic as she shouted her warning. And because I can recreate that sound with such digital fidelity in my mind, it's a memory that always fills me with that same stomach-dropping sense of dread I felt two years ago. I have literally just felt that same fight-or-flight shot of adrenaline coursing through my blood as I type these words.

So, when I said I can laugh about it now, maybe I was wrong.

Because right now I don't feel like laughing.

All I can feel is sweat on the back of my neck.

At any rate, how does a man who feels responsible for the safety of his family react in such a situation? A man's house is his castle, after all, and someone was trying to storm that castle. What's more, in that castle live innocent women and children—that is, everything in the man's kingdom worth protecting. (I actually only have one woman living in my home but women sounded better for that last sentence to be grammatically correct.) I can't speak for everyone who's faced a similar circumstance, but this particular man did the only thing that crossed his mind in that moment.

He didn't race for his handgun. He didn't grab his knife. He grabbed a souvenir baseball bat.

You know what I'm talking about. The only thing I could think of in the panic of that moment was not a real, thirty-four-inch baseball bat (which we have in the garage), but instead one of those roughly eighteen-inch, brightly colored, and *small* souvenir replica baseball bats they sell at major-league baseball parks and memorabilia stores to children. Yeah. One of those. And to make the "weapon" look as nonthreatening as humanly possible, the bat had a little string to hang it coming out of the handle. If memory serves, we had gotten it as a gift for letting some smoke-detector company give us a presentation in our home. It wasn't worth it. They stayed forever. But at least now I had a bat that wouldn't scare off a preschooler. So, there's that.

I also have a pretty good idea what you're thinking right about now: What good is a kiddie souvenir baseball bat when you're defending your family against someone who's up to no good?

This is the part I can laugh at now.

As it turned out, the souvenir bat did the trick with the would-be intruder.

And it may have also saved my life.

❧

How a Kid's Souvenir Bat May Have Saved My Life.
Here's why the children's bat still has a special place in our house—and in our lives.

Still dressed in the red gym shorts and nothing else save for the souvenir baseball bat in my hands, I head down our stairway as quickly as my legs will carry me.

I should also mention that as the glass started shattering our monitored house alarm started going off. And I called a neighbor and asked for help. He did nothing. Just watched from his backyard over the fence. He said it was just some druggie and we'd be fine. Lucky guy I am with neighbors like that. (For the record, I would have jumped the fence and tackled that idiot to protect my neighbor's young family—or maybe even drawn my gun on the person and held him or her there until the police arrived. The intruder, not my "fearless" neighbor. Yes—that was sarcasm.)

I run toward the glass doors. I scream my most guttural battle cry. I brandish the bat over my head. Then I think better of it and run back toward the front door to open it so that any neighbors still at home can see what's going on. And I position myself there. Guarding the bottom of the stairs from anyone getting upstairs to my family.

And staring out of the front door with eyes that would scream "help me" to anyone passing by. With each *whack*, I could hear more glass shattering over the sound of the alarm.

My hope was that once the intruder got in and looked up and saw a crazy, half-naked man with a small club in his hands, he or she would reconsider his or her endeavor. After all, this crazy man had a look in his eyes showing that he wasn't willing to go down without a fight.

Suddenly, the intruder stopped beating on the glass door. The house was silent except for an ear-piercing alarm sound. Almost too quiet. Was he or she inside? I didn't know. She wasn't.

She had turned and fled.

§

Our intruder, it turned out, was a twenty something-aged woman. (And, this is just reporting a fact that people who are both willing and able to break into your house are both scary and dangerous no matter their gender.) As it turned out, the woman had selected our house in a case of mistaken domicile identity. As the police would later explain, she "thought" she was at a neighbor's house two doors down from ours. I put the word "thought" in quotes because the woman was in a drugged-out state, looking for some crystal methamphetamine (or something—I'm hardly an expert on the kinds of drugs that cause people to want to smash through sliding glass doors with their bare hands) that the neighbor had "stolen" from her. He had picked her up at a bar in the middle of the night and brought her home. She was a transient. Heavyset, pierced from head to toe, including her eyes, tattooed from head to toe, she looked like hell. I saw her a little while later when I tried chasing her down through the neighborhoods to catch her—a story for a later day or another book.)

Further, as I would eventually learn from the police, she had almost been *arrested* earlier in the day—like three-o'clock-in-the-morning earlier—for assault with a deadly weapon. As for my "brilliant" neighbor who brought her home—yes, more sarcasm—she had tried to stab him and steal his drugs. And apparently, she actually did stab him, as I heard from the police. But he was fine. We were not. But she had fled so she wouldn't get caught after the stabbing and now wanted her drugs back. (Did I mention the police said she was high on meth and something else?)

Put simply, the woman was a meth addict. And for that, she receives my sympathy and my forgiveness. And the promise that if she ever makes that mistake again, I will have my gun pointed squarely at her, and she won't be lucky enough to get away. I hope that she has since banished the personal and situational demons that led to her becoming addicted to drugs and making dangerous decisions. She is lucky I grabbed the bat. Lucky to be alive. I don't take kindly to people putting my family in danger and had I grabbed my gun I would have headed rapidly for the backdoor and shot first and asked questions later. But I didn't.

That said, she scared the hell out of us Gallaghers that morning. And we still have moments when we think we hear a sound out back and jump and race for the door and the panic button. And the gun.

OK. Yes. I still haven't really told you about the bat.

But I still haven't fully fleshed out the souvenir baseball-bat part, and how it saved my life. The tiny bat helped me theoretically protect my family from the drug addict trying to break in, yes, but it also came in handy as the police arrived, looking for the intruder.

Here's how it went down:

Erica had arrived at our bedroom door to let me know of our intruder with phone in hand. So, while I was scrambling for the bat and heading downstairs to meet our would-be intruder, Erica had already dialed 911. She was on the phone with the police requesting help while at the same time gathering up Jaden and Jensen to huddle in the master bedroom. We also have a can-be-ferocious dog Hailee that could have helped me, but as silly as this sounds, I made Erica keep Hailee upstairs because I didn't want her getting hurt. I was going to face this challenge alone.

Now, as I've already mentioned multiple times and a somewhat ironic detail in this episode's third act is that I actually have a conceal license to carry a firearm. And I do, in fact, keep a firearm under lock and key in our bedroom closet. (As it turns out, people who get carry-and-conceal licenses don't go to all that trouble unless they are indeed gun owners.) In other words, I *should* have tried to grab my firearm before heading downstairs. But I grabbed the souvenir bat instead. Brilliant.

I've never been in combat, but I can certainly empathize with a phenomenon known as the "fog of war." The fog of war refers to the intense stress of combat situations that causes brains and plans (both on an individual and collective level) to short-circuit. Obvious things are missed. The best-laid plans are completely forgotten. And in the intense stress of that moment, the one thing I was supposed to remember just...slipped my mind. I can't explain it. We were all in a state of panic. We were all caught off guard. It was so sudden and unexpected. It's easy to talk a big game but once you are thrust into that situation and you feel your family is in danger, your mind just gravitates toward anything you can grab, anything at all, to protect them and do it quickly. The gun safe was locked because I don't want my kids getting hold of the gun for obvious reasons. I felt I had to act fast and my mind only led me to the bat conclusion. Or maybe it was God who led me to that conclusion as you will see.

In any event, one of the first things you're taught when you have a carry-and-conceal license is to *always* describe yourself to the police anytime you call for help. After all, the police must contend with their own fogs of war when dealing with 911 calls, and one of the things they need to sort out under tremendous strain and commotion is who are the good guys and who are the bad guys.

Here are the four things the police knew about the 911 call that morning:

1. There was an intruder at our house.
2. The intruder may be armed and dangerous.
3. There were women and children being threatened.
4. There was a half-naked man in red shorts with a bat.

Notice the part about the description of the husband and homeowner? The part about how the guy in the red shorts with the baseball bat (albeit a miniature version) was one of the good guys?

Me neither.

It doesn't exist in this telling, because it didn't while it was happening. Erica was amazing in following exactly what I screamed to her. "Tell them who I am, what I am wearing exactly, that I have a bat, and that I'm the homeowner and your husband!" She did. I heard her say it. Exactly. But apparently the 911 operator was dealing with her own fog of war, and in her haste to gather the police quickly to our home, she forgot to mention what the good guy looked like. The operator only relayed to them that there was a man there with a bat matching my description and a break-in and women and children were in danger. This meant that as far as the responding officers knew, *anyone* could be the intruder they were looking for. And this shady-looking guy with the bat? Well, he was most likely him.

In fact, in their minds *I* was the intruder they were looking for.

Yes. The guy dressed only in a pair of red gym shorts, running out of the front door of the house where the 911 call had come from, gesturing at the police? For all they knew, *that* man was the dangerous intruder threatening the family inside. Or had he already hurt them?

So, there I am, bursting out of my front door, frantically summoning the police once I see them pull up. I'm motioning my left hand in a come-here gesture while holding the bat firmly in my right. As they are trained to do, the police draw their weapons and take cover behind their squad-car doors. They then begin shouting instructions at the crazy man in the red gym shorts. "Drop the weapon!"

The weapon. They saw that as a weapon. I didn't drop it. Alarm blaring and in my fog, it didn't sink in what they were saying. I kept holding it and motioning at them. They weren't coming. Why not? At this point I didn't realize that the intruder was for sure gone. I didn't know if the person was about to be inside or was in already. Was he or she about to race behind me up the stairs? Why wouldn't the police come in? What the hell were they doing? I kept motioning for them to come. They kept yelling. I didn't get it. Then I did. I looked back left and saw an officer take cover behind his open door like you would see in the movies. And *this* time I did notice something between the door and the car. I noticed his hand holding something. Something that looked like…his gun. Cocked and pointed squarely at me. They were growing impatient with my failure to comply with their verbal commands. I finally realized what they were yelling. It all sunk in. At once. And I was even more terrified.

Do you now see how me waving around a small souvenir baseball bat, rather than a loaded pistol, might have worked to my advantage?

I don't even like to give much thought to what might have been that morning if, in my efforts to protect my family, I had remembered my gun. I choose to think about an image I can now laugh at—an image of a half-naked man waving a small kiddie baseball stick at the police, shouting and pointing for them to *come at me,* as it appeared I was doing.

Then again, laughing over terrifying moments is a luxury afforded to those who live to tell the tale. I almost didn't. I was the victim of two terrifying events that morning. So maybe I'm still not quite at the point of laughing about it yet. And retelling this makes me wonder if the yet will ever come.

The Value of Protection
But as I've just outlined, had I simply run outside holding a gun in my hands, I may not be here to tell the tale. This might have been a story told by someone else, probably some mainstream-media activist about the risks in gun ownership, and why gun owners are more likely to be killed by gunfire than non–gun owners. I'm not trying to make a statement that's anti–Second Amendment; I'm actually in favor of it. I'm just letting you know that my decision on when to brandish my firearm and when it might put me at more risk is being carefully considered.

After the home-intruder episode, Erica and I beefed up the security around our house. In hindsight, we probably went too far. We upgraded our alarm system and added additional external alarms so that our neighbors (not the two I've previously mentioned) can be aware of any peril we may be in. And we always leave it set, even when we are home during the day. We've installed razor wire at the top of our fence just below line of sight so it doesn't look like Alcatraz. And diagonally across the fence. If someone tries to jump our fence again to break in, they may not live to get to our sliding glass door. And of course, we always inspect our glass break sensors for any service needed. And we've taken other precautions as well. I thought several times about how a person's house is his or her castle, and I even did a Google search on "home moats." Erica and our damn HOA say no. For now.

By the way, moats are actually a thing, especially for the doomsday preppers and some high-net-worth individuals among us. My favorite quarterback, Tom Brady, for example, has a moat around his house. (It probably won't surprise you to learn that he and I are in different tax brackets, however.) I just keep telling myself that moat isn't to keep crazy fans like me out.

But here's the deal. A terrifying event like what happened on that spring morning two years ago—well, it changes you. Once you go through the trauma and stress of something like that, you start making plans for the next time someone comes beating at your door.

Events like that leave emotional scars. They affect your peace of mind.

In the world of living in a house and sleeping soundly through the night, there really isn't much we can do about events that affect our peace of mind. Sure, we can install security systems, live behind fences, and even under the protection of police forces that are the most prepared and professional on the planet. But even all of that is only minimal control. We all still get alarmed by the creak of a floorboard, the thump of a bird landing on our roof, or other small bumps in the night.

In the world of investing, however, true peace of mind is much more attainable. The markets can rattle and thump and groan all they want, and you can still sleep like our one-year-old Jensen (at the time) who slept through most of the home-intruder incident.

For now, I just want things all safe and familiar. My life may not be perfect, but it is what I have known.

—Ann M. Martin, *A Corner of the Universe*

Your Financial Security System

For those approaching retirement, the story of the home intruder should invoke memories of two traumatic financial events: 2002 and 2008. These two episodes where forces beyond the average investor's control tried to smash through the metaphorical home of their retirement plans were very destructive for many. Each of these years—the S&P indexes were down 22 percent and 38 percent, respectively— taught investors some very painful (and long lasting) lessons about the value of protecting their money.

These two events *should* leave investors asking themselves this question: What will I do if something like 2002 and 2008 tries to break into my retirement accounts in the coming months or years?

Security measures for houses are not realistic—or even necessary—in every situation. You may not choose to own a gun, or install razor wire, or pay for a monitored security alarm. Heck, I know people who *don't lock their doors,* and consider *that* a security measure. (The thinking is that people who really *want* to break in will anyway, and things can be replaced, but people can't. I don't agree with that thinking, but there it is. After all, what if the thief walks in through the unlocked door and harms those people? Doesn't that logic fall apart?)

Fortunately, protecting your investments from risk in the US stock market isn't all that complicated. It's something that almost any investor can and, in my opinion, *should* do. The only exception is the very young, just starting out investor building his or her first $10,000 to $20,000 in their portfolios.

For everyone else, you can protect your investments essentially with a single word:

Diversification.
Diversification is easy to explain. It simply describes a risk-management strategy that mixes a wide range of investments in a portfolio. Why diversify? Reliability. Stability. Consistency. A *diverse* portfolio will, on average, yield higher returns while simultaneously posing a reduced risk of loss than any individual investment within the portfolio.

What Diversification Doesn't Look Like
Real-estate holdings, for example, can be a great addition to your overall portfolio. But a million-dollar portfolio with five rental houses and $50,000 in liquid assets is *not* diversified. That portfolio is wildly overexposed to the vagaries of real-estate busts and booms. Just ask anyone who made a home purchase in 2006 whether home

values can decline. In fact, the losses in real estate *triggered* the broader economic problems that eventually wiped out banks, car companies, brokerage firms, and the S&P Index. And even in a hot real-estate market, one bad renter out of a portfolio of five—a tenant who stops paying rent that takes several months to evict, and who damages the house—can wreak financial havoc on otherwise spotless real-estate assets.

Diversification, then, means a portfolio of different kinds of investment *products.*

It means that some of your net worth is tied to the US stock market. Some is tied to global markets. Some is in bonds. Some is in annuities. And some might be other assets such as real estate or other physical property, such as gold, or art, or heck, maybe even collectible automobiles. Or collectible souvenir kiddie baseball bats. But probably not the latter.

ॐ

The point is this: we won't be able to prepare for the intruder banging at the door of your retirement plans until we sit down and talk. During our conversations, I'll be able to do a full "security audit" of your portfolio. And once we have that information in hand, then we can put in place a great security plan for your own financial castle.

But you can only do this if you *don't wait* until your financial alarm system is going off. Just like I did on the morning of the home intrusion, people tend to panic when the alarm bells are going off; when the menace is at your doorstep. My moment of panic ended harmlessly enough other than the emotional trauma for our family. God was gracious enough to have me home and not let Stabby Stabberson (that's what I'll name our drugged-up, weapon-yielding "friend") come in to face Erica and our small children alone just a few feet away. But remember that most moments of panic and poor decision making don't end as happily.

So, my parting advice in this chapter is that waiting for the next correction, or worse, a bear market—drops of 10 or 20 percent or much more—is *not* the time to install your security measures. At that point, you've already suffered a great loss. The time to install an exceptional financial-security system is *now*. And I want to be your personal installer.

You may not have five super-bowl rings like Tom Brady, but building a security moat around your investments? That, my friends, is within reach for all of us non-royalty types.

9

"IT'S FOOTBALL TIME!"

Love involves a peculiar unfathomable combination
of understanding and misunderstanding.

—*Diane Arbus*

Over the course of several conversations conducted at the Gallagher Financial Group offices, I essentially ask clients, whether new or existing, to do a bit of self-reflection. I try to get people to ponder on questions that should be at the forefront of everyone's mind when putting together a sound financial plan, or as my dad puts it (on the front page of our website, no less), to build a retirement income that he or she can never outlive.

I want people to spend a lot of time reflecting on how much monthly income they expect to have, or need, to cover their expenses. I want people to consider what their existing income levels are, how much debt they carry (I have spoken to couples at retirement age who, tragically, are burdened with over *six figures* of credit-card debt), how much they owe on their house, what kinds of insurance coverage they have, and whether they can expect to be responsible for the care of a spouse, a child, a grandchild, or perhaps even a parent.

Once we've completed that reflection process, I try to build an investment portfolio that fits with the overall picture of retirement these people have painted. For example, if they prefer a strategy that favors lower, more predictable returns over potentially higher returns with more downside exposure, I counsel them accordingly. I try to educate those kinds of investors about the products that carry the least risk.

So, as we reflect, metaphorically speaking, on the topic of reflection, I'll start this penultimate chapter with a story of literal reflection. It's a story that began as I was staring at my own reflection in a bedroom mirror, and then noticed something stuck to the periphery of that mirror that wasn't quite right.

❦

It's Football Time!

About a year ago, I stumbled across a book (I believe it was *The Compound Effect*, by Darren Hardy) whose central idea of a particular part was this: gratitude is good. It's good for you; it's good for the person who's the object of your appreciation. Gratitude comes with a host of benefits, both psychological and physiological. It's good for mental health, blood pressure, stress levels, relationship satisfaction, and many more. (As you've heard me say, I'm all about building relationships, and the one I have with Erica is the most important one I'll ever have, followed by the relationships with Jaden and Jensen. But back to Erica for a moment.)

In fact, expressing gratitude in a daily journal, as Darren Hardy suggests (and as he actually did), is a very simple, and scientifically proven method for boosting the happiness and abundance you feel.

Except daily journals are buggers to actually *write*. Life with two young children is, well…it's life with two young children, which is to say that almost every waking hour that isn't devoted to making a living for said young children is otherwise spoken for. Young children need to be driven back and forth to activities. They need dinner made. They need their clothes washed, their rooms cleaned, and so on. Hard for a guy with two young children and a bustling financial-advisory practice, to fit in much time for journaling. But what a guy *can* fit in, or at least what *this* guy has managed to fit in, is a much more convenient way to journal and show his wife appreciation.

My secret? Post-its.

That's right; I simply keep a Post-it notepad—the same ones I use all the time in my office—in my master-bathroom vanity drawer. That way, anytime a notion of thankfulness crosses my mind, I can reach into that drawer, scribble down the sentiment, and then stick the Post-it wherever it will be seen. Like the vanity mirror. I like to think that I've invented, or at least rediscovered the long-lost art of sending the "analog" version of a Tweet. Or a text.

As you might guess, all of these "paper thank-you Tweets" are directed at Erica. As you might guess, all of them end up on the vanity mirror, as this is a place that Erica is likely to visit most each day. So, if you were to break into my house right now, walk into our master bedroom, and take a picture of our vanity mirror, you'd see glass decorated with about two dozen Post-it notes. (Actually, please don't do that; your likely consequence was just outlined in my previous chapter and we could do without any additional trauma.)

And if you zoomed in on that vanity mirror, you'd see things like this written on little yellow slips of paper:

> *Thanks for getting my clothes ready for tomorrow.*
> *Thanks for making us dinner.*
> *Thanks for doing the dishes.*

And, were you to travel back in time—if you had been there to see me check on that same vanity mirror a few years ago—you might have laughed just as I did when you noticed the one note that didn't quite fit. Had you been there, you'd have seen another Post-it with three words and an exclamation mark. That one read:

> *It's Football Time!*

*The single biggest problem in communication is the illusion
that it has taken place.*

—George Bernard Shaw

When I first noticed Jaden's sticky note on the vanity mirror, I remember chuckling at the yellow outlier, which I then followed up with some fatherly over-explaining.

I called Jaden into our master bedroom, thanked him for adding his Post-it to the mirror, and then proceeded to educate him about the whole idea behind the gratitude Post-its. I told him some version of what I just relayed a few paragraphs ago: that the notes were for times when daddy wanted to show appreciation to mommy. It was for recognizing something special, or something completely ordinary that mommy had done to make our lives better. I described how the use of the Post-its wasn't for making announcements, and especially wasn't for making announcements about how excited we were about an upcoming pee-wee football game that morning. If you wanted to thank mommy or daddy for waking up at six o'clock on a Saturday morning to make breakfast and get you to your eight o'clock football game, well then that's fine, but the idea of the Post-its is to express gratitude to *others.*

The entire five-minute passing along of fatherly wisdom ran about four minutes and forty-five seconds too long.

In any event, Jaden waited until I had finished my explaining, said "Uh-huh," and then he explained that he had seen daddy writing mommy notes and he wanted to participate. And that morning he wrote it, we were in a hurry to get him to his game and mommy was helping him get ready. And he was excited. And that's what he came up with. After explaining this he left the bedroom. I stood there for a few moments longer, looking at the mirror surrounded by Post-it notes, rereading the things I had already said to Erica through my paper Tweets. My eyes settled on the large, scrawling text of a then four-year-old, and I chuckled once more.

And yes, I left the "It's Football Time" sticky note right where it was.

After all, it's Erica's favorite one.

☙

Know the Purpose.

As you've seen, the "thankful sticky note" exercise in my house has a very specific purpose. Its purpose is to express gratitude for the mundane, every day, small details about Erica. I want her to know that I notice these things. I want to remind her that she is important, that her contributions are appreciated and that her efforts are recognized. I want her to know that I don't take these things for granted.

Of course, Jaden didn't understand the purpose of the sticky notes when he took a pen, wrote the "It's Football Time!" note, and added it to the collection on our master vanity.

Then again, Jaden was four years old. It's OK not to understand the purpose of a bunch of sticky notes when you're four.

But when I do my own *reflection* on the sticky-note story, I'm reminded of what I see at work every day when it comes to the investment allocations of the clients and potential clients I interview. In almost all cases where I'm taking on a new client, I see a financial *sticky note* that doesn't fit in with the *purpose* of the overall portfolio. Or two. Or three. Or more.

In other words, the overall theme expressed to me might paint a picture of someone looking to protect his or her assets from the risk of a market downturn.

And yet, within his or her assortment of investments, I see something that might as well have been purchased by a four-year-old with a pen.

I see things like:

> An **account**—an entire IRA in some cases that is invested in one or two single stocks.

A **product** that is tied closely to the performance of a high-risk sector.

A **portfolio** where too much money is tied up in one asset class (like only bonds or only real estate).

Or something that generally just doesn't fit with the investor's stated *purpose.*

⚜

Gratitude is the healthiest of all human emotions. The more you express gratitude for what you have, the more likely you will have even more to express gratitude for.

—Zig Ziglar

When you reflect, what do you see?

As with Jaden's sticky-note outlier that caught my attention a few months back, these are the *financial* sticky notes that immediately catch my attention. As I did with Jaden (well, as I attempted to do), I then try to educate and coach new clients about why the one or more particular stickies don't fit the theme of the overall objective, which in this case is to help them retire with comfort and peace of mind.

But unlike Jaden, you won't have the luxury of shrugging your shoulders, ignoring the lecture about a thing's *purpose,* and then leaving crazy, old man Matthew Gallagher to his bedroom ruminations. (Well, of course you *can*—none of my investing advice comes with a requirement that you actually heed the advice. You *can* drink a double shot of espresso at 10:00 p.m., but I don't recommend it if you're trying to get a good night's sleep. You *can* choose to run up $50,000 in credit-card debt if you have the means to do so, but I wouldn't advise it if you're trying to fund a stable retirement.)

After all, Erica may have stepped in to save the "It's Football Time!" sticky note, but she won't be much help if you insist on holding an investment that's working counter to your retirement goals.

Erica's patience with non-four-year-olds has its limits. Even with a husband who can sometimes act like a four-year-old. Trust me on this one.

$\mathcal{Q}$

In any event, besides serving as a reminder to thank the spouse (or significant other) in your life, this chapter is all about understanding something's *purpose*.

The purpose of your retirement savings is to help you live the life you want in your golden years. The purpose of all that money is to help you travel with your spouse, see your grandchildren, give to charity, sponsor a theater troupe, learn a second language, learn to Samba, fly a helicopter, become a nature photographer, eat at every Michelin three-star restaurant on the planet, walk the steps of Angkor Wat, bungee-jump off the Victoria Falls bridge, buy a convertible Camaro, buy a beachside cabana, buy a professional sports team, or whatever other goals and aspirations you have for your money as you reach the twilight of your life.

When it comes to the goals for your retirement years, having the wrong sticky note on your financial vanity mirror isn't a cute mistake that can be chalked up to the misunderstanding of a small child.

The wrong sticky note has consequences. For example, it can mean paying hundreds of dollars a month in interest to a credit-card company instead of using a few hundred dollars a month to enjoy fine dining. And this is on the low end of the spectrum of consequences. At the extreme end, I've seen much more heartbreaking results of people having the wrong stickies around their financial mirror. I've seen couples forced into Medicaid (not Medicare) for their health-care requirements because they had run out of money. I've seen couples on Medicaid be *split up* never to see their spouse again because of available beds in long-term care facilities throughout Texas. Could you imagine something so horrible?

As reluctant as I am to alarm or upset my readers, you need to be aware of the realities and the stakes. The world can be an unforgiving place. The world will not care if you run out of money. After all, if you didn't care enough to protect what you had, why should it?

So, it's important to understand that a sticky note running counter to your stated retirement objectives can mean the loss of tens, or even hundreds of thousands of dollars. It can make it a lot more difficult to achieve your retirement dreams.

$$\mathcal{D}$$

As I've discussed previously in this book, during the initial fact-finding time spent with a client, I ask a lot of questions. I get clients to *reflect* on where they are, where they want to go, and what path will help them get there. I do this in an effort to develop as complete a financial picture as possible.

And I do this so that if I see something that doesn't quite fit into their stated financial goals, we can adjust. Working together, we can take the "It's Football Time!" sticky notes off your financial mirror, and replace them with items that better fit the theme of your retirement plan.

By ensuring that all the sticky notes share the same *purpose*, we can help you enter your retirement years with a feeling of gratitude. Gratitude for a life well lived, for financial footing well established, and perhaps, even for the Certified Financial Planner™ practitioner who helped get you there.

If you're so inclined, you can even leave me a sticky note saying so.

There's a big whiteboard in my office.

10

PARENTS KNOW BEST

*Understand that great accomplishments require
great effort. If a goal is achieved without effort, it
is no accomplishment but a mere happening.*

—Rachelle Goodrich, *Slaying Dragons*

In the first chapter of this book, I emphasized that being a Certified Financial Planner™ practitioner is less about relationships to *money* and more about relationships to *people*.

And with that in mind, I'd like to bring this title full circle with a story that, like so many others I've focused on, illustrates the kind of *person* you'll be working with should you entrust the Gallagher Financial Group for guidance on your journey to retirement.

This final story is a story about a very literal journey—a road trip that went awry. Moreover, it's a story about how the events of that journey left a lasting impression on a young man, and continues to shape the business and family life of the adult that young man became.

The journey begins with a young Matthew Gallagher (or Matt as I went by back then) whose home is in Colleyville (D-FW area), who is attending college in Edmond (Oklahoma City area for a semester), and who has a few close friends in Kansas City, Missouri. It begins with that young nineteen-year-old Freshman college student foolishly driving from Oklahoma City to Kansas City so that he can spend spring break celebrating St. Patrick's Day, only to then find himself faced with a daunting, eight-and-a-half-hour drive to return to the place where this headstrong and wayward young man should have been all along: home.

And why am I starting this story in the third person, you ask? Because upon looking back, the story is so remarkable that I still sometimes have a hard time believing it happened to me. In fact, if someone told me this story about him- or herself, I'd think he or she were making most of it up.

Yet every word about what happened to that college kid is an absolute fact.

And what the story says about that college kid's family is every bit as true.

In a Land before Time
Speaking of things hard to believe, there was once a time before cell phones.

One year of that peculiar and prehistoric era was 1999. Spring of 1999 to be exact. OK, fine, it wasn't *technically* before cell phones, but it might as well have been for almost every college kid in America, including yours truly. (And by yours truly, I mean me, which also means I'm switching this tale back to the first person now. I mean, really, who writes about him- or herself in the third person?)

So then, late one Wednesday evening, I find myself in Lee's Summit, Missouri—a suburb to the northeast of Kansas City—spending a week with friends I had met while on several Christmastime church retreats I participated in during my high-school years. As I previously stated, it was St. Patrick's Day week. Actually this particular day *was* St. Patrick's Day, and this kid from Bombay, India wasn't *about* to miss a chance to celebrate his Irish heritage (cough, cough) with his friends. After all, I've been a Notre Dame fan all my life. I don't just love my Notre Dame Fighting Irish, I *loooooove* them. Like Jaden with that Thomas piggy bank. And with my love (*looooove*) for all things Boston from the sports teams to the city itself (remember I am from that area originally when I was adopted), I was practically a dark-skinned leprechaun. A dark-skinned leprechaun from a formerly Catholic father with the last name of Gallagher. I mean, what could possibly be more Irish than all of that?

Now, did my parents approve of me driving up from Oklahoma City to see friends in Kansas City? Did they try to persuade me to spend my time more productively? Did I ignore their advice about such matters and do it anyway? Suffice to say that I listened to them about as well as you'd expect, which is to say about as well as all nineteen-year-olds who already know everything listen to their parents. When you're young and dumb, as the saying goes, you're... young and dumb. And selfish. My mom's birthday was March 19, and to commit to that week meant I knew I wouldn't be there for it when I could have been otherwise since it was spring break. Geez. Reading that last sentence even I don't like the younger me. But as I said, being young and dumb is pretty much the norm for most of us. Thank God we have all advanced from that point. Well, most of us have anyway.

After days of hanging out, we are now nearing evening on St. Patrick's Day, and I'm ready for some fun. Except that my friends are no longer able to go out because of family plans—you know, spending time with their *own* parents—and I've suddenly got nowhere to stay. Also, I haven't slept much that week as I'd already been up there six days since the previous Friday. Did I mention this was on a Wednesday night? And as for being so tired? Well, all those prayers of gratitude (cough, cough) to St. Patrick over the course of that week really take a lot out of a guy. Thus, the young and dumb college kid finds himself in one heck of a pickle. Or more correctly: I put *myself* into one heck of a pickle because I was suddenly facing one long, blankety-blank slog of a drive back home to the Dallas-Fort Worth area. A long, lonely, nine-hour drive when I could hardly keep my eyes open from all the late nights I had spent awake with friends. In the dark, no less.

Oh, and if you're now asking, *why Dallas? Why not Oklahoma City? It's a long drive, but still, it's closer than Dallas.* Here's the answer; as I mentioned earlier, not only is it St. Patrick's Day, but it's also spring break. I couldn't drive a mere five hours to Oklahoma City because I lived in the dorms, and the dorms were closed for spring break.

What's more, not only did I not have a cell phone I could use to contact someone in case of emergency during the drive, I didn't even have a CD player in my beat-up, five-speed, manual-transmission, no-cruise-control car to keep me entertained. The only thing I'd have for my trip across endless stretches of southern Kansas and northern Oklahoma were the AM radio, the FM radio (when they could get a signal), and my creeping sense of regret.

To put it mildly, the decision to drive to Kansas City for that week did not involve a great deal of *wisdom*.

೭

Dallas or Bust. Are These the Only Two Choices?
So, it was Dallas or bust on that auspicious Wednesday night. And bust is almost exactly what I did. After nearly falling asleep at the wheel and swerving across two lanes of traffic, I pulled off Interstate 35 at the next exit while still in Kansas City, Missouri. I found a pay phone (remember those?). I was scared. I was panicking. I suddenly missed the comfort of my own bed more than I thought possible. And so, like all college kids who find themselves out of their depth thanks to a combination of one part homesickness and four parts stupidity, I called my parents.

Of course, I didn't realize at the time what I was truly doing. When viewed through the prism of time, however, I know exactly what I did—in the midst of an unsteady chapter in my life, I was seeking out my *foundation*.

೭

I vividly remember the conversation from that pay phone to this day. I spent most of the time talking to my mother, and then a little to Dad. I did most of the talking. They did most of the listening. In truth, they didn't know what to say. "Just take a little at a time," Dad told me. "Be safe," Mom added just before we hung up, "and pull over to rest if you need to."

And so that's what I did.

As fortune would have it, one of those little bits of driving ended just outside of Wichita, Kansas. I fueled up the car and decided to call Mom and Dad to update them on my progress. Three hours down, I was going to say, and just six more to Dallas. (Again, recall that this was before Find My Friends, or Glympse, or really anything GPS that we now take for granted. My parents' only method of knowing my location was through *my* pay-phone calls from those lonely stretches of interstate.)

Mom picked up. Before I could get my second sentence out, she said, "Son, where are you?"

"Um, I'm just outside of Wichita."

"Oh, thank God," Mom replied. "You need to go to the airport now."

"Why?" I asked, confused. "What's at the Wichita airport?"

"Dad," she told me. "He lands in thirty minutes."

∾

If pressed for time, I can give you this whole story in one sentence:

Doc Gallagher bought a one-way plane ticket so he could drive his son home that night.

∾

The ache for home lives in all of us. The safe place where we can go as we are and not be questioned.

—Maya Angelou, *All God's Children Need Traveling Shoes*

Dad strode off the plane, extended his hand to retrieve the keys to my beat-up, five-speed college-mobile, and the two of us headed south from the Wichita airport late that Wednesday night.

It was about 11:30 p.m. I fell asleep almost immediately in the passenger's seat. When I next woke up, we were pulling into a hotel in Oklahoma City. Very early that next morning, Thursday, we got up about 5:00 a.m. and started ticking off the remaining miles into Dallas where, incredibly, *Dad kept all his day's appointments.*

As I said just a moment ago, I can get to the essence of the story in one sentence. A man bought a one-way plane ticket and drove his son home. But whenever I tell the longer, better version, the version I'm telling you now, I often pause and think about the unlikely nature of what transpired that evening. When I get to the part of Doc arriving at the airport, it's one of the few times that I can go quiet for long stretches in the middle of a tale.

I've also told you earlier that I'm a devout man, and my faith plays a central role in my life. That said, I won't call what happened that night a miracle in the strictest sense of the word, but so much had to be aligned *just right* for me to meet up with Doc in Wichita. So many what-if scenarios run through my mind. Some are obvious: What if I hadn't stopped for gas just outside Wichita? What if I had topped up in Emporia, Kansas, and decided to push on to Oklahoma City?

Other what-ifs are almost unimaginable: What if I hadn't swallowed my pride and let my parents know I was in trouble? What if I had fallen asleep, as I almost did in Kansas City, while stubbornly trying to defy my parents' advice? And the most obvious one? What if I hadn't called my parents while getting gas in Wichita just to check in because I missed them and to let them know I was OK? My dad would have been completely stranded in Wichita with no car, no cell phone, and no way home. After all, 11:30 p.m. is too late to catch a flight back to Dallas from such a place. And Mom would have had two of her boys in trouble in different locations, neither able to contact the other. So, while it's probably a little too self-regarding to consider what happened a miracle, the world's too big and mysterious to have the time to teach lessons to stubborn nineteen-year-olds; I do believe strongly that someone was looking out for me that night. God, of course, and a few of his angels.

Their names were Gail and Neil Gallagher.

𝒶

Know What Not to Say
This may surprise you as much as anything else I've said in this chapter; I don't really have any financial advice related to this story.

Sometimes in this business, knowing what *not* to say can be as important as the advice you offer.

So, as I conclude these chronicles, I won't say anything further about finances, or investments, or the economy.

What I will say is this: I was nineteen years old when Doc Gallagher drove an hour from his home in Colleyville to the Dallas Love Field airport (and left his vehicle there to pick up another day), bought a ticket while standing at the counter (which must have been very expensive), and flew from Dallas to Wichita on a *gamble* that somehow, some way, in an era before cell phones and GPS navigation, before Red Bull energy drinks and Sirius XM Radio, Gail Gallagher would be able to get in touch with her bull-headed, jackass son, Matthew, and let him know that his Dad was flying up to shepherd the son home.

I was nineteen years old. It was exactly half my lifetime ago. And yet that one evening continues to influence my outlook and actions as an advisor, as a husband, and as a father. And as a son.

In fact, my hope is that I'll be able to pass along a similar legacy of *stability* and *reliability* to my own children. Even as I write this today, at age thirty-eight (almost), I don't know that I'd handle a similar situation with my own children in the same way. I think that if Jaden or Jensen did something equally as impulsive and irresponsible, I'd use the entire trip back home as an opportunity to deliver the world's longest father-son lecture series.

But here's the thing: Dad said almost nothing to me the entire drive from Wichita to Dallas. Yet the lesson he passed along that evening was *indelible*.

I'm still working diligently toward the true north that Doc and Gail Gallagher have set for me. And I do believe I'll get there eventually. And if I accomplish nothing else in life other than to reach for those targets of *stability* and *reliability*, even if I don't sign up one single additional client in our financial-advisory practice, then I will consider my life a *smashing* success.

𝔔

The Ties That Bind

And so, this last Gallagher Chronicle is one meant to both underscore and tie together all the ones that preceded it.

It's the story of the kinds of *values* the Gallagher Financial Group was founded on. It's the story of how the foundation of the Gallagher Financial Group was laid, and how each brick has been added to that structure, one client at a time. It's the story of how this firm has been shaped over the course of thirty years. It's the story of the son who is taking over that firm.

It's about the kind of man he is still in the process of becoming. It's about the tenets he strives to infuse into the company he is now helping steward into the next thirty years. Or more.

It's a story of two generations (and counting) building and nurturing stable, reliable relationships in the financial-advice business.

Most of all, it's a story about *wisdom*.

This book is a tale of wisdom learned by a son, forged through experience, and informed by principles that have been passed from a mother and a father to a son.

𝔔

I wish you all the best in pursuit of a successful retirement. I wish you all the best in defining a legacy of your own.

My parting promise to you, the reader, is that I, along with the rest of the Gallagher Financial Group, will do everything in our power to help you define and build your own legacy as you approach your retirement years.

SOURCES

During the 2008 bear market, the average investor lost 38 percent. https://www.fool.com/investing/mutual-funds/2009/01/21/the-only-investing-strategy-for-a-bear-market.aspx

The US stock market during the recovery from 2009 to 2015 increased nearly 200 percent. https://www.nadex.com/learning-center/glossary/bearish-and-bullish-definition

However from NASDAQ's close at a five year low in June 2002, the S&P 500 and Dow closed higher and the NASDAQ posted the best first half since 2009 in June 2017. https://www.cnbc.com/2017/06/30/us-stocks-last-day-of-quarter-banks.html http://www.cnn.com/2002/BUSINESS/asia/07/10/wallst.close/index.html